The
Halogen Oven
Everyday Cookbook

The Halogen Oven
Everyday Cookbook

200 quick, easy and nutritious recipes
for your infrared, turbo, convection oven

SARAH FLOWER

SPRING HILL

This US edition is published by Spring Hill, an imprint of How To Books Ltd.
Spring Hill House, Spring Hill Road
Begbroke, Oxford OX5 1RX
United Kingdom
Tel: 0044 1865 375794
info@howtobooks.co.uk
www.howtobooks.co.uk

First published 2010
This US edition first published 2011

A catalog record of this book is available from the British Library.

ISBN: 978 1 905862 88 7

Designed and typeset by Mousemat Design Ltd

NOTE: The material contained in this book is set out in good faith for general guidance and no liability can be accepted for loss or expense incurred as a result of relying in particular circumstances on statements made in the book. Laws and regulations are complex and liable to change, and readers should check the current position with relevant authorities before making personal arrangements.

Thanks to my Mom, for teaching me the joys of cooking as a child and for helping me plan new recipes for this book.

Contents

Introduction

As a journalist, I'm fortunate enough to hear about and review new products. I had seen press releases about a new oven that was supposed to save time and money, so I was pleased when a halogen oven was sent to me from British company JML. My first thought was confusion: how on earth did this strange-looking thing work? Surely, being round, it would be limiting to use? How wrong I was!

Since then I have extolled the virtues of the halogen oven to anyone who will listen. I've never been a fan of microwaves, but the halogen oven is a completely different entity. It cooks some things up to 40 percent faster and others pretty much the same as a conventional oven. It reheats, broils, bakes, roasts, steams, defrosts and slow-cooks; it even makes toast and hard-boiled eggs. In short, it's a great machine for families as well as single people or couples, students… even vacation homes.

At home, the halogen hasn't replaced my conventional oven but it has limited its use dramatically. When I have a baking day, I use the conventional oven, making sure I fill it up to justify turning it on. However, I use the halogen in some form on most days, whether it's making a quick snack or a meal. It's also incredibly useful during the Christmas period and when we have dinner parties.

If you're new to the halogen, don't be scared of it. Treat it like a very efficient conventional oven and experiment with the timings. The glass bowl gives you a bird's-eye view of what's happening inside, and allows you to act quickly to avoid a disaster if and when necessary. The recipes in this book should give you a wide variety of ideas that you can adapt to suit your own preferences.

I have noticed that some halogen oven recipes on the internet recommend high temperatures, which reduce the total oven time. However, I have kept to a more conventional approach because I found that high temperatures often lead to burned tops and raw centers. This obsession with speed rather than the quality of the finished product is probably due to people treating the halogen like a microwave.

I prefer to reduce the temperatures so that they're similar to the approach used with conventional ovens. This allows you to create many dishes (including cakes) without a problem, while capitalizing on the fact that, because it's small and compact, the halogen uses less energy than a conventional oven, even though the timings aren't any different.

This book contains numerous recipes and tips that will help you enjoy the many benefits of the halogen oven. The recipes have come from years of cooking, as well as from friends, family, adaptation and experimentation. I adore baking cakes, so this was one area where I really wanted to prove that the halogen could cope. I soon realized that family favorites can work well in the halogen with only very minor tweaks when necessary. The more you use it, the more confident you will become.

I hope you enjoy this book and I wish you many great meals ahead.

Sarah x

Using Your Halogen Oven

You probably received your halogen oven with minimum advice on how to use it. If you're lucky, you may have a booklet containing a couple of recipes. I hope this chapter helps make life with your halogen simple and clear.

Choosing the right machine for you

There are many halogen ovens on the market, but the two main variations are the size of the bowl and whether it has a hinged lid. Choose a machine with the largest bowl you can find, since this increases the oven's usability. You can also buy extenders; these are metal rings that fit over the top of the halogen bowl, literally extending the bowl height, which allows more to fit in your oven. The lid then fits on top of the extender. Extenders are also useful if you want to keep food away from the heating element to prevent burning. Personally, I think it's better to buy a halogen oven with a hinged lid if you can afford it—definitely a safer and easier option.

How do they work?

The halogen oven is basically a large glass bowl with an electric halogen lid. The lid is heavy because it contains the halogen element, timer and temperature settings. The element heats up the bowl and the fan moves the air around the bowl to create an even temperature. Because it's smaller than a conventional oven, it heats up faster, reducing the need for long preheating—and in some cases reducing the overall cooking time.

This makes it a popular choice for those on a budget, living by themselves, or (like me) cooking for a busy family. It has even become popular with college students and motor- and mobile-homeowners. I read on a forum that some motor-/mobile-homeowners use the self-clean facility just like a mini-dishwasher —ingenious! It also makes a good second oven and really becomes invaluable at busy times like Christmas or dinner parties.

Compared to conventional ovens, halogen ovens cook in a slightly different way, so learning to use it often involves a process of trial and error. For example, the lid's handle has to be in place for the machine to turn on. This means that when you lift the lid, the oven automatically turns off. However, if you have favorite recipes that you cook in a conventional oven, just try them in the halogen. Cooking at a slightly lower temperature or for less time normally produces the same results—and hopefully this book will give you more confidence.

The halogen oven isn't a microwave and doesn't work in the same way, so if you think you can cook food in a few minutes by using it, think again. It does, however, have a multitude of functions: defrosting, baking, broiling, grilling, roasting and steaming are all perfect for halogens. Remember that, for maximum benefit, air needs to circulate around the bowl, so ideally place dishes and trays on racks and don't be tempted to overfill.

Getting the right equipment
This sounds obvious, but make sure you have oven trays, baking sheets and casserole dishes that fit inside your halogen oven. There is nothing more frustrating than planning a meal and at the last minute realizing that your dish doesn't fit in the machine! You can use any ovenproof dish or tray: metal, silicon and Pyrex are all fine. The halogen oven is round, so it makes sense to look for trays and stands that are of the same shape but smaller so that you can remove them without burning yourself.

When I first started using the halogen, 80 percent of my bakeware didn't fit it. A quick purchase of accessories proved invaluable (check eBay or garage sales if you're on a tight budget). You can also buy an accessories packagethat contains steamer pans, browning trays, broiling pans, toasting racks and even an extension ring. These are highly recommended if you use your oven regularly A general internet search should point you in the right direction; Amazon is always a great place to start.

Let there be light
As experienced halogen users will know, the halogen light turns on and off during cooking. This isn't a thermostatic fault, as some people have mentioned in online forums. It simply turns off when the desired temperature is reached, then on again when it drops. Just set the temperature and marvel at how quickly the oven reaches the required temperature: literally in minutes. I love the light; there's something quite cosy about walking into your kitchen on a winter or fall evening, seeing the glow of the halogen oven and watching your food cook.

Timings
Most halogen ovens come with a 60-minute timer and temperature setting dials. All halogens turn off when the timer settings have been reached. This means you can be sure that if the phone rings or you're called away from the kitchen, your food won't be ruined.

Size
The oven is small enough to sit on a countertop, but you do need to allow space for removing the lid if it isnt hinged. The lid can get very hot and, being the brains of the machine, it's fairly large and heavy, so it's a good idea to buy a lid stand. Be careful when using this, however, since it can seem quite flimsy until you get used to it. You could opt to place the lid on a heatproof surface, but again: be careful not to burn yourself—or your countertop!

Easy does it

Your oven should come with some tong-type gadget to help you lift out the racks. This is OK, but I also use a more substantial set of tongs. Just as with any oven, the bowl and its contents get very hot, so wear oven mitts: they'll cover your whole hand and wrist and can prevent accidents. And of course, don't let your children near the halogen when it's in use.

Defrosting

Most halogen ovens have a defrost facility, which is very useful; refer to your manufacturer's details. Many people want recommended timings for defrosting, but it really depends on what you're defrosting and how big it is. Try setting the defrost button to five- or ten-minute intervals and testing as you go.

I don't really buy frozen dinners, but judging by comments on internet forums, this is a popular choice for halogen owners. When cooking frozen meals, remember that the nearer the food is to the element, the browner it will get—and the higher the temperature, the quicker it could burn! Don't panic: one of the joys of a halogen oven is the ability to see the food clearly through the glass bowl so, if in doubt, watch the food to prevent it from burning. See Chapter 2 on snacks for more information and advice.

Aluminum foil

Some people like to use aluminum foil when cooking. This can be a good idea because it prevents food from browning too quickly, or it can be used to "parcel" foods, but make sure the foil is secure. The fan is very strong, and if the foil isn't fixed, it could float around the oven and might damage the element. Another way to prevent burning is to turn down the temperature or place the food further away from the element (use the low rack or add an extension ring).

Cleaning your oven

The halogen is promoted as "self-cleaning." This basically means that you fill it with a little water, a squirt of dishwashing liquid and turn on the wash setting. The combination of the fan and the heat allows the water to swish around the bowl, cleaning it in about 10 minutes. Personally, I think it's just as easy to remove the bowl and put it in the dishwasher. It always comes out gleaming.

The lid is a little trickier to clean, so I'd refer to the manufacturer's guidelines since each product can be a little different. Whatever you do, don't get the element or any other electrical parts wet!

How to cook

Individual chapters in this book provide details of how to cook different types of food in your halogen. You can follow the recipes to the letter, or see if you can create your own by using those provided as guidance.

If you're concerned about cooking meat, I'd advise using a meat thermometer. If the temperature is too high, then meat or roast will brown quickly on the surface, but it may not be cooked in the middle. Don't panic too much. You'll soon get used to it.

High and low racks

Two standard racks are supplied with every halogen oven: a high rack and a low rack. The high rack is positioned nearer the element, so use this if you want to brown something. The low rack is used when you need a longer cooking times.

You can also cook directly on the bottom of the bowl. I do this fairly often, particularly if I'm being lazy and just want to pop in some oven fries. This method does cook well, but takes a little longer compared to the racks because air isn't able to circulate all around the food.

Baking

Some people avoid using the halogen to bake cakes but I think this is because they set the oven temperature too high, which results in a crusty brown cake top with a soggy middle. Setting the oven to a lower temperature can solve this problem. Muffins and cupcakes take between 12 and 18 minutes. You only really encounter problems with cakes if you bake for too long at too high a temperature. Try some of my cake recipes and you'll see how simple it can be.

Preheat or not to preheat

Most recipes I've found on internet forums don't mention preheating the halogen oven before cooking anything. This is due probably to the speed with which the oven reaches the desired temperature setting. However, I still think it's worth turning the oven on five minutes before use, just to bring it up to the right temperature. This helps a lot—especially when you're cooking something like soft-boiled eggs that need a definite time period. Some machines feature a separate preheat button, but with others you just have to set the required temperature and turn the machine on as usual.

Weights and measures

I'm constantly being asked for my cake recipes and it always throws me because I never measure anything when I bake! My husband laughs when he sees me in the kitchen, literally throwing in all sorts of ingredients, seemingly oblivious to the end result. Thankfully, they all come out perfectly tasty!

Don't follow my lead, though—at least not until you're confident using your halogen. Measure as you go. There's some great measuring equipment available which will make life easier.

Measuring cup

I use a glass Pyrex measuring cup. They're very hardy, easy to read and come up gleaming after every wash—unlike plastic cups which can stain. Measuring cups are ideal for measuring liquids or mixing ingredients together and they're easily available at supermarkets or online. I have also picked up various pieces of "kitchenalia" from garage sales and auctions over the years.

I hope this chapter hasn't confused you. Move on to try some recipes and then come back to this chapter at a later date—it will probably make more sense then!

Enjoy!

Snacks

Although we all aim to be healthy, there are times when a quick and easy snack really hits the mark. Unlike microwaves, halogen ovens can heat up pastries, pizzas and snacks without resulting in a soggy mess. They can also make delicious toasted sandwiches with ease. Here are some suggestions to inspire you.

Toast

This is really where the accessories for halogen ovens come into their own. If you buy an accessory pack, you should get a breakfast rack—a metal rack with some compartments for your eggs. However, here I've just used the high rack.

- Simply put your slices of bread on the high rack.
- Cook at 475°F for about 4–6 minutes until the toast reaches the desired color. The toast should brown on both sides without you needing to turn it.

This is a trial-and-error recipe. When I first tried it, some of the slices were toasted but not golden; they tasted the same but the odd slice lacked color. I adjusted the temperature setting and then things improved.

Toasted Cheese

Because the halogen oven has a powerful fan setting, you don't have to toast one side of the bread before adding your topping. You can have delicious toasted cheese in 5 minutes.

- Take two slices of bread and cover them with the grated cheese of your choice. Season to taste.
- Place on the high rack, topping face upwards.
- Cook at 475°F for 5–7 minutes until the topping is bubbling. Serve open-face or together for a toasted cheese sandwich.

Toasted Sandwich

- Place one slice of bread with your chosen topping and one plain slice side by side on the high rack.
- Cook at about 475°F for 4–5 minutes, until the topping is bubbling.
- Place the plain bread slice over the topped slice to form a sandwich and cook for a further 1–2 minutes if necessary.

Welsh Rarebit

- Preheat the halogen oven using the preheat setting or set the temperature to 475°F.
- Place the slices of bread on the high rack for 3–4 minutes to toast.
- Meanwhile, put the milk, butter, cheese, and mustard in a saucepan on your stove top and heat gently, stirring, until dissolved and thick. Be careful not to have this too high or it will stick and burn.
- Spoon the cheese mixture on one side of the toast and season to taste. Place back on the high rack and cook for another 3 minutes, or until golden and bubbling.
- Serve with a side salad and some delicious chutney.

2–4 slices of bread
3–4 tablespoons milk
1 tablespoon butter
2 cups grated mature
  Cheddar cheese
1 teaspoon mustard

Egg and Cheese Rarebit

2–4 slices of bread
2–3 eggs
3–4 tablespoons milk
1 tablespoon butter
2 cups grated mature
   Cheddar cheese
1 teaspoon mustard

- Preheat the halogen oven using the preheat setting, or set the temperature to 350°F.
- Place the eggs in the egg rack or on the high rack and cook for 7–8 minutes until they are soft or medium. (The egg rack comes with the accessory pack. It is specially designed and is higher than the low rack.)
- Meanwhile, in a saucepan on your stove top add the milk, butter, cheese, and mustard, heat gently and stir until dissolved and thick. Be careful not to put it over too high a heat or it will stick and burn. Remove from the heat, cover and set aside.
- Remove the eggs and turn up the halogen's temperature to 475°F. Put the slices of bread on the high rack and cook for 3–4 minutes to toast.
- Remove the eggshells and roughly slice them directly onto the toast, especially if the egg yolk is still soft.
- Spoon the cheese mixture onto the egg slices and season to taste. Put back on the high rack and cook for 3–4 minutes until golden and bubbling.
- Serve with a side salad and some delicious chutney.

Mozzarella, Tomato and Basil Toastie

This is one of my favorite quick snacks. You can leave it open-face or covered to make a toasted sandwich—the choice is yours! If I don't have any fresh basil leaves, I add some baby spinach leaves.

- Preheat the halogen oven using the preheat setting, or set the temperature to 475°F.
- Create your toastie by putting the tomatoes on buttered or unbuttered bread (depending on your preference). Add some basil or spinach leaves and cover with mozzarella. Season to taste.
- Place on the high rack and cook for 3–4 minutes until the cheese is golden and bubbling.
- Drizzle with a little olive oil. Serve with a side salad.

Note: For extra zing, spread a little pesto on the bread before adding the tomatoes, leaves and mozzarella.

2–4 slices of wholewheat bread
1–3 tomatoes (depending on size and portion numbers), sliced
Fresh basil leaves (or spinach leaves)
1 ball of mozzarella, sliced or torn
Salt and black pepper, to taste
Olive oil
Pesto (optional)

Sardines in Tomato Sauce on Toast

2–4 slices of
  wholewheat bread
1 x 4.25 oz can
  sardines in
  tomato sauce
Scallions (spring
  onions), finely
  chopped (optional)
Sun-dried tomatoes
  (optional)

- Preheat the halogen oven using the preheat setting, or set the temperature to 475°F.
- Toast one side of the bread according to the instructions on page 10.
- Remove the sardines from the can and mash them slightly. (Add some finely chopped scallions/spring onions and some sun-dried tomatoes if you like). Put the sardines on the bread slices.
- Place on the high rack and cook for 3–4 minutes until golden and bubbling.
- Serve with a side salad.

Bacon

Who can resist some bacon with breakfast—or a BLT as the ultimate snack? You can cook bacon without adding more fat in approximately 6 minutes using the halogen oven.

- Put the bacon on the high rack.
- Set the temperature to 475°F.
- Cook for 5 minutes, then turn over and cook for another 5 minutes or until your desired crispness is reached.

Soft- or Hard-boiled Eggs

You wouldn't think a halogen oven could be used to boil an egg, but you'd surprised. You can put the eggs directly on the rack, or buy the breakfast rack as an optional accessory.

- Preheat the halogen oven using the preheat setting or set the temperature to 350°F.
- Put the eggs on the high rack or breakfast rack.
- Cook for 6 minutes to achieve a soft-boiled egg or 10 minutes for a hard-boiled egg. Be careful when removing them from the oven—they will be very hot.

Note: This didn't work when I first tried it. I discovered that you really do have to preheat the oven and it's best if the eggs are at room temperature before cooking. If they've been in a cold refrigerator, you may have to cook them for a minute or two more—you'll soon discover the timing that suits your taste.

Bruschetta

I love the simplicity of bruschetta. It really is just something on toast, but it tastes so much nicer! I use French bread, a ciabatta or thick slices of homemade bread. Experiment with your own toppings. This recipe is my favorite cheat for a quick snack.

- Preheat the halogen oven using the preheat setting or set the temperature to 475°F.
- Spread red pesto thinly over the bread slices. Add the scallions and mozzarella.
- Finish with a few cherry tomato quarters on each slice. Season to taste and drizzle with a little good-quality olive oil.
- Place on the high rack and cook for 4–6 minutes until golden.
- Serve immediately.

4–6 thick slices
   of bread
Red pesto
3–4 scallions (spring
   onions), sliced
1 ball of
   mozzarella, torn
6–10 cherry
   tomatoes, quartered
Salt and black pepper,
   to taste
Drizzle of olive oil

Garlic Mushroom and Mozzarella Bruschetta

1 tablespoon butter
2–3 garlic cloves,
 crushed
6–8 mushrooms
4–6 slices of bread
Handful of basil or
 spinach leaves,
 shredded
1 ball of
 mozzarella, torn
Salt and black pepper,
 to taste

- Preheat the halogen oven using the preheat setting, or set the temperature to 475°F.
- Melt the butter and add the garlic—you can use the halogen to do this but don't let the butter burn.
- Put the mushrooms on a baking sheet and brush them with the melted garlic butter.
- Place the tray on the high rack and cook for 5 minutes to help soften the mushrooms.
- Put the shredded leaves on the bread slices, followed by the garlic mushrooms. Finish with some torn mozzarella. Season to taste.
- Place the slices back on the high rack and cook for 5 minutes, or until melted and sizzling.

Mozzarella, Basil, and Tomato Panini

Create your own café favorite snack in your halogen.

- Preheat the halogen oven using the preheat setting, or set the temperature to 475°F.
- Slice open the panini (or similar) rolls and fill with mozzarella, basil leaves, and sliced tomatoes. Season to taste.
- Place the filled rolls on the high rack and cook for 4–6 minutes until golden and the mozzarella has started to melt. You may want to turn them halfway through.
- Serve with a side salad and tortilla chips.

2–4 panini-type rolls
1 ball of
  mozzarella, torn
Handful of basil leaves
2–3 tomatoes, sliced
Salt and black pepper,
  to taste

Cheese and Ham Panini

2–4 panini-type rolls
Mature Cheddar,
   sliced or grated,
   quantity to taste
4–6 slices of ham
Salt and black pepper,
   to taste

- Preheat the halogen oven using the preheat setting, or set the temperature to 475°F.
- Slice open the panini (or similar) rolls and fill with the cheese and slices of ham. Season to taste.
- Place the filled rolls on the high rack and cook for 4–6 minutes until golden and the cheese has started to melt. You may want to turn them halfway through.
- Serve with a side salad and tortilla chips.

Fresh Garlic Bread

You can make your own garlic bread from French bread by following this basic recipe.

1 loaf of French bread
1 tablespoon butter
1–2 garlic cloves,
   crushed (or more
   to taste)
1–2 teaspoons
   mixed herbs

- Partially slice the French bread into 1–1¼ inch thick slices, making sure you don't cut right through the bread.
- Mix 1 tablespoon of butter with 1 or 2 crushed garlic cloves and a sprinkle of mixed herbs.
- Thickly spread the butter in between the slices of bread.
- Put the bread on a baking sheet, making sure it fits into your halogen oven. Place the tray on the lower rack and turn the oven on to 450°F.
- Cook for 5–8 minutes until golden.
- To serve, simply allow the diners to tear off the bread slices.

Variation Try spreading the bread with either green or red pesto instead of garlic butter.

Frozen Garlic Bread

- Place the frozen garlic bread on a baking sheet, making sure it fits into your halogen oven.
- Place the tray on the lower rack and turn the oven on to 450°F.
- Cook for 8–12 minutes until golden.
- To serve, simply allow the diners to tear off the bread slices.

Warming Naan Bread

Naan bread is delicious with curries and Indian meals, and you can now buy it in many supermarkets, healthfood and Asian food stores. The halogen oven is a great tool for warming naan bread.

- Sprinkle the naan bread with a little cold water.
- Place it on the high rack and cook for 5–8 minutes at 450°F. You may want to turn the naan over halfway through cooking.
- Serve immediately.

Frozen Pizza

Refer to your manufacturer's cooking instructions for more information.

- Preheat the halogen oven using the preheat setting, or set the temperature to 400°F for 5 minutes while you prepare your pizza.
- Put the pizza on the lower rack. If you have an accessory pack, you could put it on the browning tray; otherwise, place it directly on the rack or use a pizza tray.
- You may want to position the upper rack upside down on the top of the pizza for the first 10 minutes. This prevents the toppings from lifting with the force of the fan and it's advisable if your pizza has lots of loose toppings. Alternatively, if your halogen has different fan settings choose a lower one.
- Set the temperature to 425°F and cook for 10–15 minutes until golden.

4 croissants
Mature Cheddar,
   quantity to taste
4–6 slices of ham
Salt and black pepper,
   to taste

Toasted Cheese and Ham Croissants

Just as with the panini, bruschetta, and toasted sandwiches, these recipes are designed to show you what you can do with the halogen. Feel free to change the ingredients to suit your palate. Why not try a sweet filling? One of my children's favorites is chocolate spread with slices of banana.

- Preheat the halogen oven using the preheat setting or set the temperature to the highest available.
- Slice the croissants in half and fill with cheese and ham.
- Place the filled croissants on the high rack and cook for 3–6 minutes until crispy and the cheese starts to melt.
- Serve immediately.

Frozen Oven Fries

If you have children or teenagers in the house, there will come a time when they want you to cook some oven fries. The halogen oven cooks these in approximately 20 minutes.

- Turn the halogen oven to 425°F.
- Place the oven fries on a baking sheet on the low rack. I sprinkle them with a touch of paprika and a pany dash of olive oil to add flavor and prevent them from drying out.
- Cook for 20–25 minutes, turning occasionally if you feel like it, until they are golden. If you use a browning tray, the fries should brown all over.

Potatoes

Baked potatoes are delicious, and in terms of running costs this is where a halogen oven excels over a conventional oven. Depending on their size, baked potatoes can be made in 40–60 minutes and, unlike cooking them in a microwave, they have a crispy skin with a delicious fluffy middle. Baked potatoes can be filled with leftover chili, spaghetti sauce, grated cheese, tuna or even (if you're British like me) baked beans.

Some people rub a little sea salt into the skins before baking potatoes; others brush them with olive oil to help crisp the skins. This is all just personal preference, so I'll leave this aspect up to you!

Cheesy Baked Potatoes

SERVES 4

4 large potatoes
1–2 tablespoons
   of butter
1 cup mature
   Cheddar, grated
1–2 carrots, grated
Dash of
   Worcestershire sauce
Black pepper to taste

With a little imagination, baked potato fillings can be so much more than a bit of grated cheese. Here's a simple suggestion to spice up the popular cheesy filling.

- Preheat the halogen oven using the preheat setting, or set the temperature to 400°F.
- Prick the potatoes all over with a sharp knife. Put them on the low rack.
- Bake the potatoes until they're soft in the middle but have crunchy skins. This normally takes around 45–60 minutes, depending on size.
- Cut the potatoes in half, scoop out the insdies and put this in a large bowl. Return the empty shells to the oven for 5 minutes to crisp.
- Meanwhile, mix the potato with the butter, cheese, carrots, Worcestershire sauce, and black pepper.
- Re-stuff the shells and finish with a sprinkling of grated cheese on top.
- Bake for another 5 minutes until the tops are golden. Delicious!

There are many possible variations to this recipe. The formula remains the same: scoop out the middle of the baked potato and mix the ingredients together, then reassemble everything and put it back in the oven to brown. The following pages contain some more suggestions.

SUITABLE FOR VEGETARIANS

Italian Baked Potatoes

SERVES 4

- Preheat the halogen oven using the preheat setting, or set the temperature to 400°F.
- Prick the potatoes all over with a sharp knife. Put them on the low rack.
- Bake the potatoes until they are soft in the middle but have crunchy skins. This normally takes around 45–60 minutes, depending on size.
- Once the potatoes are cooked, cut them in half and scoop out the middles. Mix the potato with the butter, cheese, pancetta, and oregano. Add a dash of milk if the mixture is too dry (it should be the consistency of mashed potato). Season to taste.
- Re-stuff the shells and finish with a sprinkling of grated cheese on top.
- Bake for another 5 minutes until the tops are golden.

4 potatoes
2 tablespoons butter
6 oz (scant half-pound) Gorgonzola cheese (or other bluse cheese), crumbled
6 oz (scant half-pound) pancetta (Italian bacon), chopped
1 teaspoon oregano
Dash of milk
Salt and black pepper, to taste

Sour Cream and Chive Baked Potatoes

4 potatoes
4 oz (scant ½ cup)
  sour cream
1 tablespoon chives,
  freshly chopped
½ cup mature
  Cheddar, grated
  (optional)
Salt and black pepper,
  to taste

- Preheat the halogen oven using the preheat setting, or set the temperature to 400°F.
- Prick the potatoes all over with a sharp knife. Put them on the low rack.
- Bake the potatoes until they are soft in the middle but have crunchy skins. This normally takes around 45–60 minutes, depending on size.
- Once the potatoes are cooked, cut them in half and scoop out the middles. Mix the potato with the sour cream and chives. Season to taste.
- Re-stuff the shells and finish with a sprinkling of grated cheese on top.
- Bake for another 5 minutes until the tops are golden.

SUITABLE FOR VEGETARIANS

Egg-in-the-Nest Baked Potatoes

SERVES 4

- Preheat the halogen oven using the preheat setting, or set the temperature to 400°F.
- Prick the potatoes all over with a sharp knife. Put them on the low rack.
- Bake the potatoes until they are soft in the middle but have crunchy skins. This normally takes around 45–60 minutes, depending on size.
- Once the potatoes are cooked, cut them in half and scoop out the middles. Mix the potato with the butter, cheese and chives. Add a splash of milk if the mixture is too dry (it should be the consistency of mashed potato). Season to taste.
- Re-stuff the shells. Using a spoon, make a hollow in the middle of each potato, large enough to fit in the egg. Break an egg into 4 of the potato halves, leaving 4 with just the cheese mixture.
- Bake for a further 10–12 minutes until the eggs are firm and the tops are golden.

4 large potatoes
1–2 tablespoons of butter
½–⅔ cup mature Cheddar, grated
2 teaspoons chopped chives
Splash of milk
4 eggs
Salt and black pepper, to taste

SERVES 4

4 sweet potatoes,
   scrubbed
½ cup mature
   Cheddar, grated
Salt and black pepper,
   to taste
Splash of milk

Baked Sweet Potato

If you have never tasted a baked sweet potato, I urge you to
try one—they really are delicious. I love adding a little bit of
grated cheese and serving these with a portion of baked
beans: it makes a very simple but very wholesome and healthy
meal. Why not look at the baked potato recipes in this chapter
and use sweet potatoes instead or create your own recipe?

- Preheat the halogen oven using the preheat setting,
  or set the temperature to 400°F.
- Prick the potatoes all over with a sharp knife.
  Put them on the low rack.
- Bake the potatoes until they are soft in the middle
  but have crunchy skins. This normally takes around
  45–60 minutes, depending on size.
- Once the potatoes are cooked, cut them in half and
  scoop out the middles. Mix the potato with the
  cheese and seasoning. Add a dash of milk if the
  mixture is too dry (it should be the consistency of
  mashed potato).
- Re-stuff the shells. Bake in the oven for 10–12
  minutes until the tops are golden.

SUITABLE FOR VEGETARIANS

Baked New Potatoes

This must be the simplest recipe of all!

- Preheat the oven using the preheat setting or set the temperature to 425°F.
- Put the potatoes in the halogen bowl along with the olive oil, garlic, herbs, and paprika. Stir well, ensuring the potatoes are all coated. This will give them a vibrant red-gold color.
- Bake in the oven for approximately 35–45 minutes until golden. Simple!

SUITABLE FOR VEGETARIANS AND VEGANS

2¼ lb new
   potatoes, washed
Splash of olive oil
2–3 garlic cloves,
   crushed
2–3 teaspoons mixed
   herbs (fresh or
   dried)
2–3 teaspoons paprika
Salt and black pepper,
   to taste

SERVES 4

4–6 large potatoes,
   peeled and cut
   to size
Oil of your choice
   (I use olive or
   sunflower)
3–4 teaspoons farina
2–3 teaspoons paprika

Delicious Roasted Potatoes

Who can resist a roasted potato?

- Preheat the halogen oven using the preheat setting
  or set the temperature to 425°F.
- Peel and cut the potatoes ready to roast.
- Put the potatoes in a saucepan on your stove top and
  steam or boil them for 10 minutes. While they cook,
  add the oil (about 1 inch deep) to a roasting pan and
  put it on the low rack. Alternatively, add the oil to the
  base of the halogen oven, but since the air doesn't
  circulate on the base, you'll need to increase the
  cooking time.
- Drain the potatoes and return them to the saucepan.
- Sprinkle the farina and paprika on the potatoes.
  Cover the pan and shake for a few seconds to coat.
- Add the potatoes to the hot roasting oil —be careful
  not to splash.
- Roast for 50–60 minutes (more if using larger
  potatoes), turning regularly to ensure an even,
  crisp coating. When you turn the potatoes,
  add more paprika.

SUITABLE FOR VEGETARIANS AND VEGANS

Garlic and Rosemary Roasted Potatoes

These have a fantastic flavor.

- Preheat the halogen oven using the preheat setting, or set the temperature to 425°F.
- Peel and cut the potatoes ready to roast.
- Put the potatoes in a saucepan on your stove top and steam or boil them for 10 minutes. While they cook, add the oil (about 1 inch deep) to a roasting pan and put it on the low rack. Alternatively, add the oil to the base of the halogen oven, but since the air doesn't circulate on the base, you'll need to increase the cooking time.
- Drain the potatoes and return them to the saucepan.
- Sprinkle the farina on the potatoes. Cover the pan and shake for a few seconds to coat.
- Add the potatoes to the hot roasting oil—be careful not to splash. Add the garlic cloves, onion wedges and rosemary leaves, ensuring they are evenly distributed.
- Roast for 50–60 minutes (more if using larger potatoes), turning regularly to ensure an even, crisp coating.

SUITABLE FOR VEGETARIANS AND VEGANS

SERVES 4

4–6 large potatoes, peeled and cut to size

Olive oilt

3–4 teaspoons of farina

1 garlic bulb, cloves separated and peeled

1–2 red or Spanish onions, cut into wedges

3–5 sprigs of fresh rosemary

4–6 potatoes, cut
  into chunks
1 tablespoon olive oil
1–2 teaspoons paprika

Potato Wedges

Don't waste your money on horrible frozen potato wedges—try making your own instead. Not only are they cheaper, they taste so much better!

- Preheat the halogen oven using the preheat setting, or set the temperature to 475°F.
- Place the potato chunks in a bowl with the olive oil and paprika, ensuring the potatoes are evenly coated.
- Transfer the potatoes to a baking sheet or simply place them on the bottom of the halogen.
- Cook for 25–30 minutes until golden, turning occasionally.

Variations: Add chopped garlic, chilies or herbs of your choice for extra taste.

SUITABLE FOR VEGETARIANS AND VEGANS

Cheese Crunch New Potatoes

These are really tasty—but be warned: they're addictive!

- Steam the new potatoes, still in their skins, until tender.
- While the potatoes are steaming, mix the garlic, Parmesan, dried onion, chives and olive oil together. Season to taste.
- Preheat the halogen oven using the preheat setting or turn the temperature to 400°F.
- Place the potatoes on a lightly oiled ovenproof dish, making sure this fits in your halogen.
- Using a potato masher, very gently push down on each potato to slightly flatten it. Place a small amount of the cheesy mixture on each potato.
- Put the potatoes on the low rack and cook for 15–20 minutes until golden.

SUITABLE FOR VEGETARIANS AND VEGANS

2¼ lb new potatoes
2–3 garlic cloves, crushed
⅛–½ cup grated fresh Parmesan
1–2 tablespoons dried onion
1 teaspoon dried chives
2–3 tablespoons olive oil
Salt and black pepper, to taste

Fan Potatoes

SERVES 4

4–6 medium or
   large potatoes
2–3 garlic cloves,
   crushed
4 teaspoons butter
   (or, if vegan,
   a dairy-free spread)
2–3 teaspoons paprika
1–2 teaspoons
   mixed herbs
Salt and black pepper,
   to taste
Drizzle of olive oil

These are a great favorite of my dad's and make a good alternative to roasted or baked potatoes. You can coat them with any herbs or spices and they are great with fresh chilies. This recipe is more restrained, however, and uses mixed herbs and garlic.

- Preheat the halogen oven using the preheat setting, or set the temperature to 400°C.
- Wash but don't peel the potatoes. Put them on a chopping board and use a sharp knife to cut thin slices into the top two-thirds of each potato, stopping one-third up from the base so that the potato remains intact. Slice all of the potatoes in this way.
- Rub butter over the top of the potatoes, pushing a little between the slices if you can without breaking them.
- Sprinkle with the garlic, followed by paprika and mixed herbs. Season to taste.
- Put the potatoes on a baking sheet and drizzle with a little olive oil—not too much!
- Place on the low rack and cook for 20 minutes. As the potatoes cook, they will open out slightly. If you want each slice to be golden, add a little more butter or herbs halfway through cooking.
- Lower the temperature to 350°F and cook for another 25–30 minutes until golden.

SUITABLE FOR VEGETARIANS AND VEGANS

Cheesy Dauphine Potatoes

SERVES 4

A classic dish that never fails to impress—if you aren't concerned about calories, that is!

- Preheat the halogen oven using the preheat setting, or set the temperature to 400°F.
- In a bowl, mix the garlic, sour cream, and milk until combined thoroughly. Season with the nutmeg, salt and pepper.
- Grease an ovenproof dish, and then start to make layers of potato slices followed by a little grated cheese. Place a little of the sour cream mixture between each layer, leaving the majority to pour over the top layer.
- Continue making layers, finishing with the sour cream and a little grated cheese and black pepper.
- Place in the oven on the low rack and cook for 50–60 minutes, until the potatoes are cooked. If the top starts to look too brown, cover the dish with foil.

SUITABLE FOR VEGETARIANS

1 lb 2 oz potatoes, very finely sliced
2 garlic cloves, crushed
1½ cups sour cream
½ cup milk
Pinch of grated nutmeg
Salt and black pepper, to taste
¾ cups grated Gruyère or mature Cheddar cheese

SERVES 4

4–5 potatoes, mashed
2 tablespoons butter
1 cup mature
    Cheddar, grated
Salt and black pepper,
    to taste
4 eggs
1½ cups oats
3 cups fresh bread
    crumbs
2 tablespoons
    dried onions
½ cup fresh Parmesan
    cheese, grated
4 tomatoes, sliced

Cheesy Mashed Potato, Egg, and Tomato Pie

I found this recipe in an old 1920s' British cookbook and have adapted it to suit our tastes. It works perfectly in the halogen oven—although it's a good idea to make the mashed potatoes the night before (simply double what you're making for another meal) in order to have it ready for this dish.

- Cook and mash the potato. Add the butter and the Cheddar and season to taste.
- Preheat the halogen oven using the preheat setting, or set the temperature to 400°C.
- Grease an ovenproof dish before adding the mashed potato. Break the eggs onto the potato.
- Mix the oats, bread crumbs, dried onion, and Parmesan cheese together. Season to taste.
- Cover the eggs with a layer of the breadcrumb mix. Add a layer of sliced tomato and finish with another layer of bread crumbs. Add a couple of small pats of butter.
- Place on the low rack and cook for 20–25 minutes until golden.

SUITABLE FOR VEGETARIANS

Easy Cheesy Tortilla

This is an ideal dish for using up any leftover cooked potatoes.

- Preheat the halogen oven using the preheat setting, or set the temperature to 400°F.
- In a large bowl, beat the eggs well. Add the remaining ingredients and combine.
- Pour this mixture into a well-greased ovenproof dish.
- Put on the low rack and cook for 20–25 minutes until firm.
- Serve hot or cold with salad.

SUITABLE FOR VEGETARIANS

SERVES 4

5 eggs
1 bunch of scallions (spring onions), finely chopped
2–3 medium potatoes, cooked and sliced or cubed
½–¾ cup grated mature cheese (i.e. Cheddar or Parmesan)
1 teaspoon fresh thyme (optional)
Salt and black pepper, to taste

3–4 large potatoes,
  sliced into fries
Olive oil spray
  (or other nonstick
  cooking spray)
Paprika (optional)
Sea salt

Homemade Golden Fries

Who can resist fries? These are made using spray oil so you can cut down on the amount of fat, making it a guilt-free indulgence. (I pour olive oil in a disused spray container since it's cheaper than buying store-bought spray oils.)

- Preheat the halogen oven using the preheat setting, or set the temperature to 425°F.
- Put the potatoe slices in a bowl of water for a few minutes. Drain, then steam or boil for 5 minutes.
- Meanwhile, spray the baking sheet with olive oil. (I use the browning tray for this because it helps to brown the fries all over.) Drain the potatoes and put them on the baking sheet in a single layer. Spray with a little more olive oil and sprinkle with paprika (this is optional but it helps to create a golden color and nice flavor).
- Put on the low rack and bake for 10–15 minutes, then turn the fries over, spray them again and bake for another 10–15 minutes, or until they are cooked. The cooking times depend on the thickness of the fries.
- To serve, sprinkle with sea salt.

SUITABLE FOR VEGETARIANS AND VEGANS

Sweet Potato Fries

- Preheat the halogen oven using the preheat setting, or set the temperature to 425°F.
- Steam or boil the sliced potatoes for 5 minutes.
- Meanwhile, spray the baking sheet with olive oil. (I use the browning tray for this because it helps to brown the fries all over.) Drain the potatoes and put them on the baking sheet in a single layer. Spray with a little more olive oil and sprinkle with paprika (this is optional but it helps to create a golden color and nice flavor).
- Place on the low rack and bake for 10–15 minutes, then turn the fries over, spray them again and add the chili flakes. Bake for another 10–15 minutes or until they are cooked. Cooking time depends on the thickness of the fries.
- To serve, sprinkle with sea salt and more chili flakes if desired.

SUITABLE FOR VEGETARIANS AND VEGANS

3–4 large sweet potatoes, sliced into fries
Olive oil spray (or other nonstick cooking spray)
Paprika (optional)
Fresh or dried chili flakes
Sea salt

Meat

4

The halogen oven can cook meat slightly quicker than a conventional oven, but you must be careful to get your temperature settings right. Too high and the tops of the roasts or birds will burn while the middle may remain raw or undercooked. I advise using a temperature gauge to test your meat, particularly poultry or thick cuts of meat, until you're more confident.

When meat is placed on the lower rack, it allows the juices and fats to drain away, which makes for a healthier dish. Some people worry that meat will dry out too much but, to be honest, it tends to be very tender and moist when cooked in the halogen oven—unless you overcook it, of course! If you're concerned, you can always place the meat on a baking sheet, or even cook it on the base of the halogen—ideal if you also want to roast potatoes.

You can cook a roast just like you would in a conventional oven—roughly 20–25 minutes per pound at 350°F and add another 10 minutes to the end of the cooking time. Obviously, thicker and heavier cuts of meat will require more cooking time per pound, so consult your usual recipe book as a guideline.

Make sure you leave adequate space between the element and the meat—ideally at least 1-1¼ inches. The nearer food is to the element, the more likely it is to burn or cook quickly. If you're concerned, wrap some foil over the meat for the first half of the cooking time, but check that it's secure, since it can be lifted off by the power of the halogen's fan.

SERVES 4–6

1 roasting chicken
1 red or
 Spanish onion
1 lemon
2 tablespoons butter
1–2 teaspoons
 dried tarragon

Roast Chicken

Chicken is a family favorite, and this is a great way to cook your Sunday roast. Don't forget to add your roasted potatoes (choose one of the recipes from Chapter 3).

- Preheat the halogen oven using the preheat setting, or turn the temperature to 475°F.
- Wash and prepare the chicken according to your own preference. I place a whole red onion and a lemon, both cut in half, in the cavity of the bird to enhance its flavor. I then rub the skin with butter and sprinkle with herbs, but you can place herb butter under the skin if you like.
- Place the chicken, breast-side down, on the lower rack for 25 minutes.
- Turn the bird back over so that the breast side is up, reduce the temperature to 400°F and cook for another 40 minutes, or until done—the cooking time obviously depends on the size of the bird. Always make sure the meat is thoroughly cooked before eating.
- Any fat will have drained to the base of the halogen oven—you can use some of this to make gravy.

Roast Beef with Horseradish

SERVES 4–6

A great family roast. Serve with roasted potatoes, steamed vegetables and homemade gravy.

- Preheat the halogen oven using the preheat setting, or set the temperature to 400°F.
- In a mixing bowl, combine the sugar, syrup and horseradish sauce. Season well with black pepper.
- Put the beef in a roasting pan and place it on the low rack. Cook for 20 minutes, then turn down the temperature to 350°F.
- Coat well with the sticky horseradish sauce and cook for a further 20 minutes for every pound. If the meat starts to darken too much, cover it securely with aluminum foil.
- Halfway through the cooking time add the red wine—it will mix with the beef juices and can be used for your beef gravy.
- Once cooked, wrap the meat in foil and leave it to rest for at least 20 minutes. Use this time to make the gravy. Simply combine the meat's natural juices from the roasting pan with a little cornstarch to thicken them.
- Serve with roasted potatoes and steamed vegetables.

2 tablespoons dark brown sugar
2 tablespoons maple syrup
4 tablespoons horseradish sauce
Black pepper
1 x beef roast, such as eye of round (usually around 3 lb)
$1\frac{1}{4}$ cups red wine

3–4 garlic cloves,
   crushed
½ teaspoon
   chilies, chopped
1 teaspoon
   dried rosemary
2–3 tablespoons
   olive oil
Salt and black pepper,
   to taste
1 leg of lamb
2 sweet potatoes
6–8 potatoes
2–3 teaspoons paprika
2–3 teaspoons farina
2 red onions
2–3 tablespoons
   olive oil
2–3 sprigs of
   fresh rosemary

Roast Leg of Lamb with Roasted Vegetables

A great roast or one-pot meal. Note: if you want the juices to drain away, then put the lamb and vegetables directly on the rack, but if want to roast everything in the juices, use a roasting pan or tray.

- Preheat the halogen oven using the preheat settings or set the temperature to 450°F.
- Mix together the garlic, chili, dried rosemary, olive oil, and seasoning to form a paste. Rub this over the leg of lamb. You can score the flesh first to help give the paste something to hold onto.
- Put the meat in a roasting pan and put this on the lower rack. Cook for 15 minutes.
- Meanwhile, cut the potatoes to size and steam or parboil them in a saucepan on your stove top for 10 minutes. Drain and then return them to the empty saucepan. Add the paprika and farina. Cover and shake to fluff up and coat the vegetables.
- Arrange the potatoes around the lamb and brush them with olive oil. Cut the onions in half and put them with the vegetables. Add the sprigs of rosemary.
- Cook for another 10 minutes at 450°F, then reduce the temperature to 350°F and cook for another 30–45 minutes, or until both the meat and potatoes are cooked to your satisfaction. (Exact cooking times depend on the size of the leg of lamb.) Remember to turn the lamb and vegetables regularly and brush with oil or paste as required.

Stuffed Pork Loin

SERVES 4–6

A great family roast—serve it with roasted potatoes, vegetables and homemade gravy.

- Preheat the halogen oven using the preheat setting, or set the temperature to 400°F.
- In a mixing bowl, add the bread crumbs, onion, garlic, bacon, pine nuts, sun-dried tomatoes, and chopped herbs. mix well and season to taste.
- Place the stuffing on the meat and roll tightly. Use water-soaked string to tie the loin securely.
- Rub the skin with olive oil and sprinkle with sea salt and black pepper.
- Put the loin on a baking or roasting tray on the low rack, or directly on the rack if you want the juices to drain. Cook for 20 minutes, then turn down the temperature to 350°F and cook for 30 minutes for every pound. If the meat starts to brown too much, cover it securely with aluminum foil. Use a meat thermometer to check that the meat is done, or check the juices—if they're running clear, it should be cooked through.
- Leave the pork to rest for 10–15 minutes before carving.

1½ cups fresh bread crumbs
1 red or Spanish onion, finely chopped
2–3 garlic cloves, finely chopped
4–6 strips of lean bacon, chopped
½ cup pine nuts
6–8 sun-dried tomatoes (in oil), chopped
Handful of fresh herbs (sage, thyme, oregano or parsley), chopped
Salt and black pepper, to taste
1 x 2–3 lb boneless pork loin
Olive oil
Sea salt
Black pepper

Chicken Burgers

1 onion, chopped

1–2 garlic
cloves, crushed

1 stick of
celery, chopped

½ yellow pepper,
chopped

1 lb (about 3½ cups)
ground or finely
shredded chicken

2 tablespoons of
pine nuts

1 tablespoon
homemade
wholewheat bread
crumbs

Forget fast-food restaurants; why not make your own?

- Put all the ingredients in a food processor and
  mix thoroughly.
- When mixed, form into balls: these should be firm
  but moist. If the mixture is dry, add some beaten egg.
- Use the palm of your hand to flatten the balls into
  burger shapes. Refrigerate them until ready to use, or
  freeze them in layers (separate each layer with wax
  paper to prevent them from sticking together).
- When ready to cook, brush the meat lightly with olive
  oil. Turn the halogen oven to 475°F, put the burgers
  on the high rack and cook for 4–5 minutes on each
  side until golden. (You're actually grilling them at
  this heat!)
- Serve with wholewheat buns, a salad garnish
  and mayonnaise.

Leftover Chicken Pie

This is my mother's recipe. Now that we've grown up and flown the nest, my parents have had to adapt to cooking for two instead of four. This meal is made from the leftovers of the Sunday roast, so they usually eat it early in the week.

- Heat the oil in a pan and fry the onion. Add the celery, mushrooms, cooked chicken and ham if you are using it. Cook for 3–4 minutes.
- Add the soup and heat for a further 3 minutes.
- Place the mixture in an ovenproof pie plate, first making sure that it fits in your halogen oven.
- Roll out the pastry to a size larger than required. Wet the edges of the pie plate with milk or water. Cut thin strips of pastry and place them around the edge of the pie plate. Dampen again with milk. This will give the top pastry something to hold on to. Cut the top pastry to size and place it over the pie. Crimp and seal the edges thoroughly.
- Put on the low rack and set the temperature to 400°F. Cook for 20–30 minutes until the pie crust is golden.

Drizzle or spray
  of olive oil
1 onion, chopped
2 sticks of
  celery, chopped
¾ cup mushrooms,
  quartered
2–2½ cups
  cooked chicken
1 can condensed
  chicken or
  mushroom soup
1 package ready-to-use
  puff pastry sheets
  (enough to cover
  the top of
  your casserole)

A drizzle or spray
of olive oil
1–2 garlic cloves
2 leeks, finely chopped
6 scallions (spring
onions), finely
chopped
2½ cups cooked
chicken pieces
1⅛ cups whole
button mushrooms
1 cup white wine
1¼ cups chicken stock
1 teaspoon cornstarch
1 teaspoon paprika
1 cup French beans
1 teaspoon dried
tarragon (or
a handful of
fresh tarragon)

Chicken and Mushroom Casserole

A wholesome meal that everyone loves.

- Heat a little olive oil in a frying pan and cook
  the garlic, leeks, and scallions for 2–3 minutes.
  Add the chicken and the mushrooms and cook for
  another 5 minutes.
- Place the chicken mixture in a casserole dish, first
  making sure it fits in the halogen oven. Add the wine
  and stock to the dish.
- In a cup or bowl, mix the cornstarch with
  2 teaspoons of water to form a smooth paste, then
  add this to the casserole.
- Add all the remaining ingredients. If you're using
  fresh tarragon, add half now and retain half to add
  during the last 10 minutes of cooking.
- Cook at 350°F for 35–40 minutes. If the casserole
  starts to form a skin on top, cover the casserole, or
  wrap a piece of aluminum foil securely over the top
  of the dish.

Note: If you prefer a creamier sauce, add some low-fat
Greek yogurt 5 minutes before serving.

Chicken Italiano

The flavors of this dish are delightful. There is a vegetarian version of this recipe in Chapter 6.

- In a large frying pan, fry the onion and garlic in a dash of olive oil for 2 minutes. Add the red pepper and cook for another 2 minutes.
- Add the chicken, bacon, and paprika. Stir, cooking gently for 5 minutes.
- Add all the remaining ingredients. Cook for another couple of minutes.
- Pour this into a casserole dish that fits in the halogen oven. Cover the pan with a lid and cook at 350°F for 35–40 minutes.
- Serve with small roasted or sauté potatoes and a green vegetable.

SERVES 4

Splash of olive oil
1 onion
2–3 garlic
   cloves, crushed
1 red pepper, diced
4 chicken breasts,
   boneless or pieces
3–4 strips of
   bacon, diced
2 teaspoons paprika
1 x 14.5 oz can
   chopped tomatoes
2 teaspoons sun-dried
   tomato paste
1 cup red wine
1 cup stock or water
1½ cups button
   mushrooms
Small handful of fresh
   basil, chopped
Salt and black pepper,
   to taste

Red Pesto Chicken Parcels

SERVES 4

4 chicken breasts
Butter
4–8 teaspoons of
    red pesto
1 red or Spanish
    onion, sliced
4 tablespoons of
    white wine
Seasoning

Such simplicity! If you want to include some roasted or mini roasted potatoes, choose a recipe from Chapter 3.

- Preheat the halogen oven using the preheat setting, or turn on to 400°F.
- Cut out four squares of aluminum foil, each one twice the size of each chicken breast. Grease each square with a little butter.
- Place 1 chicken breast in the middle of each square. Add 1–2 teaspoons of red pesto to each chicken breast. Cover with some onion slices.
- Drizzle with a tablespoon of white wine. Season well and secure into a parcel.
- Place on the low rack and cook for 30–35 minutes until the chicken is done.

Sticky Chicken Drumsticks

Finger-lickin' good!

- Place all the ingredients apart from the chicken in a bowl and mix well.
- Score the drumsticks with a sharp knife to give the marinade something to hold onto.
- Have a large freezer bag ready—this can get messy! Place the drumsticks in the freezer bag with the marinade and shake well to ensure that they are thoroughly coated. Secure and leave in the refrigerator overnight.
- When you're ready to cook, put a baking sheet under the high rack to catch any drips. Turn the oven on to 450°F.
- Place the drumsticks on the high rack. You can put them directly on the rack or, if you prefer, use a baking sheet.
- Cook the chicken gently on both sides, adding marinade as you go if you prefer. The advantage of cooking the chicken straight on the rack is the oven's ability to cook all sides, but you'll still need to turn the drumsticks over to get them evenly browned. Cook until the chicken is thoroughly done—this should take about 15–20 minutes depending on the size of the drumsticks.
- Serve with salad.

SERVES 4

3 tablespoons maple
  syrup or honey
1 tablespoon mustard
1 tablespoon
  Worcestershire sauce
1 tablespoon soy sauce
2 teaspoons paprika
4 chicken drumsticks

3–4 sirloin steaks
2–3 garlic cloves
Splash of olive oil
Black pepper
   to taste

Grilled Steak

This makes a quick and easy meal when served with
a delicious side salad.

- Prepare your steaks as you would normally. I rub
  mine with garlic and olive oil, then season them with
  black pepper.
- Place the steaks directly on the high rack.
- Set the temperature to 475°F and cook for 8–10
  minutes. Reduce or increase the temperature to
  achieve your desired taste—this timing is perfect for
  a medium rare, 1–1½-inch thick steak.

Hamburgers

Forget the fast-food chains. Homemade burgers not only taste better, they're also much healthier.

- Put the onion and garlic into a large bowl and stir well. Add the beef and bread crumbs and mix thoroughly.
- Add the beaten egg, coriander, cumin, mustard and tomato paste. Season to taste.
- Mix thoroughly and form into balls—these should be firm but moist. Use the palm of your hand to flatten the balls into burger shapes.
- Place the burgers in the refrigerator until you are ready to use them, or freeze them in layers (separate the layers with wax paper to prevent them from sticking together). When you're ready to cook them, brush them lightly with olive oil. Turn the halogen oven to 475°F. Place them on the high rack and cook for 5–8 minutes on each side until golden. (You're actually grilling them at this heat!)
- Garnish with salad and serve with wholewheat buns.

Variation: If you like them slightly spicy, why not add some chopped chilies and 1 teaspoon of curry powder to the burger ingredients before mixing? You could also brush the burgers with chili oil instead of olive oil to add a tasty zing.

1 onion, finely chopped
1 garlic clove, crushed
1¾ cups lean beef mince
1 tablespoon fresh wholewheat bread crumbs
1 egg, beaten
1 teaspoon coriander
1 teaspoon cumin
1 teaspoon mustard
2 teaspoons tomato paste
Salt and black pepper, to taste

Lamb and Apricot Casserole

SERVES 4–6

A drizzle or spray
  of olive oil
1 onion, chopped
2–3 garlic cloves,
  crushed
1¾ cups lamb, diced
3 teaspoons harissa
  paste or hot
  chili paste
2 teaspoons
  powdered cinnamon
1 cup red wine
1 x 14.5 oz can
  chopped tomatoes
1¼–2 cups hot water
  or stock
1 x 15.5 oz can
  garbanzo beans,
  drained
½ cup dried
  apricots, chopped
Fresh cilantro leaves,
  to garnish

A delicious lamb casserole with a small kick to liven things up.

- Heat the oil in a frying pan and cook the onions, garlic, and lamb for 2–3 minutes.
- Add the harissa or chili paste and stir well for 2 minutes.
- Turn the halogen oven to 400°F. Make sure your casserole dish fits comfortably in your oven.
- Place the lamb mixture in the casserole dish. Add all the remaining ingredients and mix well. Cover with the casserole lid, or cover securely with aluminum foil.
- Place on the low rack and cook for 50 minutes.
- Serve, garnished with cilantro leaves.

Cashew, Walnut, and Mushroom-stuffed Chicken

This is a really simple dish to prepare, but it tastes fabulous!

- Preheat the halogen oven using the preheat setting, or turn the temperature to 400°F.
- Using a food processor is the best and quickest way to make this dish. Use it to chop the nuts, mushrooms, and onion. Place these in a bowl and mix in the garlic. mix well.
- With a sharp knife, cut a slit in the side of each chicken breast to form a pocket. Stuff the mixture into these pockets, then wrap each breast in bacon to secure them.
- Place the chicken breasts on a greased ovenproof dish. Drizzle with a little oil and season to taste.
- Place on the low rack and cook for 30–35 minutes until the chicken is cooked.

⅛ cup cashews
¼ cup walnuts
1 cup chestnut, portobello or other brown mushrooms
1 onion
2–3 garlic cloves, crushed
4 chicken breasts
8 strips of bacon
Olive oil
Salt and black pepper, to taste

Spicy Chicken Wings

1–2 chilies,
 finely chopped
2 garlic cloves,
 finely chopped
2–3 teaspoons chili
 sauce (mild or hot,
 depending on
 your tastes)
Juice and zest of
 1 lemon
1 teaspoon paprika
1 teaspoon allspice
½ teaspoon ginger
½ teaspoon
 chili powder
1 tablespoon
 brown sugar
2 teaspoons maple
 syrup or 3
 teaspoons honey
10–12 chicken wings
Salt and black pepper,
 to taste

A really simple dish that takes minutes to prepare. Marinate overnight or for at least one hour before cooking. Serve with rice and salad for a great summer supper.

- In a bowl, combine all the ingredients apart from the chicken wings.
- Add the chicken wings to the bowl, ensuring they are thoroughly coated with the mixture. Cover with plastic wrap and leave to marinate overnight or for at least 1 hour. (If the bowl isn't big enough, put the marinade and wings into a large freezer bag and shake until covered.)
- Preheat the halogen oven using the preheat setting, or set the temperature to 400°F.
- Tip the wings and the coating onto a baking sheet or ovenproof dish (if you don't have the browning tray). Cook on the low rack for 20 minutes, or until the chicken is cooked.
- Serve with rice and salad.

Moussaka

Using low-fat sour cream instead of a white sauce is not only quicker, but it saves some calories.

- Place the eggplant slices in a pan of boiling water for 2 minutes. Remove and pat dry with paper towels. Set aside.
- Meanwhile, heat a little olive oil in a frying pan and fry the onions and garlic. Add the ground lamb and cook until brown.
- Add the tomatoes, tomato paste, mint, cinnamon, and seasoning and cook for another 2–3 minutes.
- Select an ovenproof dish—I normally use a Pyrex or lasagne dish for this. Make sure it fits into your halogen oven. Preheat the halogen using the preheat setting or set the temperature to 400°F.
- Put a layer of lamb in the ovenproof dish, followed by a layer of eggplant. Continue alternating lamb and eggplant, finishing with a layer of lamb.
- Mix the sour cream with the grated cheese and pour it over the final layer of lamb. Garnish with a sprinkle of grated cheese.
- Place on the low rack and cook for 20–25 minutes until bubbling.

2–3 eggplant, sliced
Olive oil
1 onion, finely chopped
2 garlic cloves, crushed
1¾ cups ground lamb
1 x 14.5 oz can chopped tomatoes
2 teaspoons tomato paste
1 teaspoon dried mint
2 teaspoons cinnamon powder
Salt and black pepper, to taste
1¼ cups low-fat sour cream
½ cup mature grated chesse, such as Cheddar or Parmesan

Quiche Lorraine

¾ cup all-purpose flour
¼ cup cold butter
5–6 tablespoons
   cold water
1 cup milk
3 eggs
½ teaspoon dry mustard
Pinch of cayenne pepper
1½ cups grated
   Gruyère or
   Swiss cheese
1 small onion,
   finely chopped
½ cup cooked ham or
   lean bacon, diced
Salt and black pepper,
   to taste

When making tarts, quiches, or pies, bake the pastry shell first because this prevents that horrible "soggy-bottom" scenario. Personally I prefer using wholewheat flour to make a savory pastry, but it's entirely up to you.

- First make the pastry. Put the flour in a large bowl and add small pieces of the chilled butter. Using your fingertips, rub the butter into the flour until the mixture resembles bread crumbs. Add the water, a little at a time, and mix until a dough is formed. Wrap the dough in plastic wrap and place in the refrigerator to cool until needed.
- Preheat the halogen oven using the preheat setting, or set the temperature to 400°F.
- Roll out the pastry on a floured surface to the size and thickness needed to line a 9-inch greased pie plate. Place a sheet of parchment paper over the pastry and cover with pie weights or dried beans.
- Bake on the low rack in the halogen oven for 10 minutes. Remove the weights (or beans) and parchment and cook for an additional 5 minutes. Remove the pie shell from the oven and reduce the temperature to 375°F.
- Meanwhile, mix the milk and eggs thoroughly before adding the dry mustard and cayenne pepper. Add the cheese, onion, and bacon or ham. Season well before pouring into the pie shell.
- Bake on the low rack for 30–40 minutes, or until golden and the center is firm. If the top starts to get too dark, cover with foil, making sure it is secure.

Ham and Leek Cheesy Bake

Ham and cheese work so well together—and this recipe proves that point!

- Cut the leeks to about 4–5 inches long and steam them for 5–8 minutes until tender.
- Meanwhile, melt the butter gently in a saucepan on medium heat. Add the flour or cornstarch and stir well with a wooden spoon. Add the milk, a little at a time, stirring continuously to avoid lumps.
- Switch to a whisk and continue to stir over medium heat until the sauce begins to thicken. The whisk will help eradicate any lumps. Add more milk as necessary to get the desired thickness—the sauce should have the consistency of custard or pudding mix.
- Add the cheese and mustard, and stir well. Season with black pepper.
- Remove the leeks from the steamer and wrap a slice of ham around each one. Lay them in the base of an ovenproof dish—a lasagne dish is good for this, but make sure it fits well inside your halogen oven.
- Preheat the halogen by using the preheat setting or set to 425°F.
- Pour the cheese sauce over the wrapped leeks. Combine the bread crumbs, oats, and Parmesan cheese and sprinkle over the leeks.
- Place on the low rack and cook for 15 minutes until golden and bubbling.

4 leeks, trimmed
2 tablespoons butter
1 tablespoon all-purpose flour or cornstarch
2–3 cups milk
¾ cup mature cheese, such as Cheddar
½ teaspoon English mustard
Black pepper to taste
8 slices of lean ham
2–3 tablespoons fresh wholewheat bread crumbs
2 tablespoons rolled oats
2 tablespoons grated Parmesan cheese

1 onion, finely
    chopped
2–3 garlic cloves,
    finely chopped
A spray of olive oil
1 red bell pepper,
    finely chopped
    (optional)
1¾ cups lean
    ground beef
½ cup plus 2
    tablespoons red wine
¾ cup finely chopped
    mushrooms,
    (optional)
3–4 fresh tomatoes,
    chopped (or 1 x 14.5
    oz can chopped
    tomatoes)
Mixed herbs to taste
Salt and black pepper
    to taste

Lasagne

Everyone loves lasagne—and the good news about this recipe is that you can speed up the cooking process by using fresh pasta sheets, or boil the dried lasagne sheets for 8–10 minutes before adding them to the dish. This will cut the cooking time down by about 15 minutes.

- Fry the onions and garlic in a little olive oil until soft and translucent. Add the chopped peppers if using.
- Add the ground beef and cook until browned, then add the wine and mushrooms (if using). Cook for 2 more minutes.
- Add the fresh or canned tomatoes, stirring well. Finally, add the herbs and season to taste. Simmer for 5 minutes.
- While the tomato sauce is simmering, make the white sauce. Melt the butter gently in a saucepan on medium heat (not high!). Add the flour or cornstarch and stir well with a wooden spoon. Add the milk, a little at a time, stirring continuously to avoid lumps.
- Switch now to a whisk. Continue to stir over medium heat until the sauce begins to thicken. The whisk will also help eradicate any lumps. Add more milk as necessary to get the desired thickness. The sauce should have the consistency of custard or pudding mix. Add the mustard, if usuing and season with black pepper.
- Preheat your halogen oven using the preheat setting or set the temperature to 400°F.

- Spoon a layer of tomato sauce into the bottom of your lasagne dish (first make sure it fits into your halogen), then pour in a thin layer of white sauce, followed by a layer of lasagne sheets. Continue alternating the layers, finishing with the white sauce. Don't overfill the dish; otherwise the lasagne may spill out during cooking.
- Sprinkle grated cheese over the top.
- Place on the low rack in the halogen oven and cook at 400°F for 40–50 minutes (or 30 minutes if using fresh or pre-boiled pasta sheets) until golden and the pasta sheets are cooked. If the top starts to get too brown, cover with aluminum foil, making sure it's secure.
- Serve with salad and garlic bread.

For the white sauce
2 tablespoons butter
1 tablespoon all-
   purpose flour or
   cornstarch
2–3 cups milk
$\frac{1}{4}$ teaspoon mustard
   (optional)
Black pepper to taste

Sheets of lasagne
Grated cheese,
   to garnish

Drizzle of olive oil
10–12 shallots,
   whole (or small red
   onions, quartered)
2 garlic cloves,
   crushed
2½ cups whole
   button mushrooms
2 carrots, diced
2 celery stalks,
   finely sliced
1 lb chicken breast
   or thigh pieces
1 lb lean bacon,
   chopped
1 x 14.5 oz chopped
   tomatoes
1 cup red wine
1 bay leaf
Handful of chopped
   parsley
2–3 sprigs of fresh
   thyme
Salt and black pepper,
   to taste

Coq au Vin

A hearty traditional dish, perfect for a winter evening.

- Preheat the halogen oven using the preheat setting or set the temperature to 400°F.
- Put the oil, shallots, and garlic in an ovenproof casserole dish. Place in the halogen oven on the low rack and cook until the onion starts to soften.
- Add the mushrooms, carrots, celery, and chicken pieces and cook for another 5 minutes. Then add all the remaining ingredients. mix well and season to taste.
- Cover with a casserole lid or double-wrapped aluminum foil, securely fastened.
- Place back on the low rack and cook for 40–50 minutes until the vegetables and chicken are cooked to taste.

Chicken, Bean, and Tomato Pot

SERVES 4

A very simple, wholesome, and filling dish.

- Preheat the halogen oven using the preheat setting, or set the temperature to 400°F.
- Drizzle the oil in a roasting pan or casserole dish that fits inside your halogen. Add the onion, pepper, garlic, chicken, and tomatoes. Drizzle with a little more oil to ensure the ingredients are well coated. Add the thyme and sprinkle with paprika.
- Place on the low rack and cook for 15 minutes.
- Remove from the oven and add all the remaining ingredients. mix well.
- Place back in the oven and cook for another 20 minutes, or until the chicken is cooked to perfection.

Olive oil
2 red or Spanish onions, cut into small wedges
1 red pepper, sliced
3–4 garlic cloves, finely chopped
4 boneless chicken breasts, halved
½ lb of cherry tomatoes, whole
Handful of fresh thyme (or 1–2 teaspoons dried)
2 teaspoons paprika
2 cups chicken stock
2–3 teaspoons sun-dried tomato paste
1 x 14–15 oz can cannellini beans, drained
Salt and black pepper to taste
Small handful of fresh parsley, finely chopped

Corned Beef and Potato Tart

SERVES 4

¾ cup plus 2
   tablespoons all-
   purpose flour
3½ tablespoons
   cold butter
5–6 tablespoons
   cold water
3–4 potatoes, cooked
   and mashed (you
   can use leftover
   mashed potato)
1 x 12 oz can
   corned beef
1 onion, diced
1–2 teaspoons
   Worcestershire sauce
1 egg, beaten
Salt and black pepper,
   to taste

I prefer to bake the pastry shell before adding the corned beef
and potato mixture.

- To make the pastry: put the flour in a large bowl and
  add small pieces of the chilled butter. Using your
  fingertips, rub the butter into the flour until the
  whole mixtre resembles bread crumbs. Add the water
  (a little at a time) and mix until a dough is formed.
  Wrap the dough in plastic wrap and place in the
  refrigerator to cool until needed.
- Cook and mash the potatoes.
- Put the corned beef, mashed potato, and diced onion
  in a bowl and mix thoroughly. Add the
  Worcestershire sauce and beaten egg and season well.
- Preheat the halogen oven using the preheat setting,
  or set it to 400°F.
- Roll out the pastry on a floured surface until even.
  Grease a pie plate, then line it with the pastry and
  trim to size. Bake blind by placing a piece of baking
  parchment over the pastry, adding baking weights or
  dried beans and cooking on the low rack for
  10 minutes.
- Remove the weights/beans and parchment and add
  the corned-beef mixture.
- Place back on the low rack and bake for 25 minutes.

Bacon and Gorgonzola Parcels

I love cabbage leaves stuffed with delicious flavors. Feel free to make your own variations to this tasty recipe.

- Place the cabbage leaves in a pan of boiling water for 2–3 minutes to soften. Remove and pat dry with paper towels.
- Put some of the bacon, onion, and Gorgonzola in the center of each leaf, season with black pepper, then roll into a parcel. Use a wooden cocktail stick to help secure the leaves in place if needed.
- Put each cabbage parcel on a greased square of aluminum foil. Bring the sides of the foil up to form a well. Add 2 teaspoons of water, then secure the foil to form a parcel.
- When all the cabbage leaves are parcelled, you can put them in and around other food, or place them together on the low rack of your halogen. Cook at 450°F for 15 minutes.
- Unwrap and serve.

8–12 large
   cabbage leaves
4 strips of
   bacon, chopped
1 small red or
   Spanish onion,
   finely chopped
⅛–½ cup Gorgonzola
   (or other blue
   cheese), crumbled
Black pepper to taste
Water

Puffed Sausage Rolls

Sausage meat
  (removed from
  its casing)
Puff pastry
Beaten egg
A sprinkle of sesame
  seeds (optional)

- Roll the sausage meat into a thumb-thick length.
- Roll out the pastry so that it is just over twice as wide as your roll of sausage meat, and half an inch longer at each end.
- Place the sausage mix ½–¾ inches from the long edge of the pastry.
- Coat the edges of the pastry with beaten egg before folding it over the sausage meat. Press down firmly on the edge before cutting the sausage rolls to the desired length.
- Preheat the halogen oven using the preheat settings, or turn on to 400°F.
- Put the sausage rolls on a baking sheet. Brush with beaten egg and sprinkle with sesame seeds before placing on the low rack and baking for 20–25 minutes until golden brown.

Variations: For a great variation to the standard sausage roll, mix some herbs with the sausage meat to create delicious Herby Sausage Rolls. If you like things hot, mix your sausage meat with some fresh chilies and a dash of Tabasco sauce to create tempting Hot, Hot, Hot Sausage Rolls. Vegetarians can opt for any of the above by using vegetarian sausage mix.

Spicy Meatballs in Rich Tomato Sauce

Serve this with spaghetti for a delicious and filling dish. Meatballs can be made in advance and frozen, and the tomato sauce can also be cooked in advance and stored in a jar in the refrigerator or frozen.

- Combine all the meatball ingredients (except the olive oil) in a bowl and mix thoroughly.
- Form the mixture into small balls and place on a baking sheet. Cover the balls with a sheet of plastic wrap and refrigerate for 30 minutes.
- Preheat your halogen oven using the preheat setting, or set the temperature to 400°F.
- Put the meatballs in the bottom of an ovenproof dish, first making sure it fits in your halogen oven. Drizzle with a little olive oil and place on the low rack for 15 minutes, rolling or turning halfway through.
- Meanwhile, combine the tomatoes, garlic, sugar, salt, olive oil, and basil leaves.
- Remove from the oven and add the tomato sauce. Reduce the temperature to 350°F and place the meatballs in sauce back in the oven for another 15 minutes before serving with some spaghetti.

Note: You can freeze the meatballs raw. I normally place them, still on the baking sheet, in the freezer until they are firm, before removing them from the tray and putting them in a freezer bag. This way they won't stick together and you can pull out the required number of meatballs as and when you need them.

Meatballs

1¾ cups ground beef
1 small onion, finely chopped or grated
1 teaspoon paprika
1 teaspoon cumin
1 chili, finely chopped
1 teaspoon chili powder
2 teaspoons Worcestershire sauce
1 teaspoon fresh parsley
1 cup fresh bread crumbs
1 egg, beaten
Salt and black pepper, to taste
Drizzle of olive oil

Tomato sauce

1 x 14.5 oz can of chopped tomatoes (or 1 lb chopped fresh tomatoes)
2 garlic cloves, crushed
1 teaspoon sugar
½ teaspoon salt
Handful of chopped fresh basil leaves
Drizzle of olive oil

Bacon, Leek, and Macaroni Cheese Bake

SERVES 4

1¾ cups dried
   macaroni
2–3 leeks,
   finely chopped
6–8 strips of bacon,
   roughly chopped
Drizzle of olive oil
2 tablespoons butter
1 tablespoon
   all-purpose flour
   or cornstarch
2–3 cups milk
¾ cup grated mature
   Cheddar cheese
½ teaspoon mustard
Black pepper to taste
2–3 tablespoons
   fresh wholewheat
   bread crumbs
2 tablespoons
   rolled oats
¼ cup Parmesan
   cheese

You can make this in advance and just pop it in the halogen to heat it up. However, make sure the sauce isn't too thick when you add it to the mixture; it will thicken further when standing and again when cooking.

- Pur the macaroni in boiling water and cook until tender (refer to the instructions on the package).
- Meanwhile, gently fry the leeks and bacon in a little olive oil or butter. Once cooked, set aside.
- Melt the butter gently in a saucepan on medium heat. Add the flour or cornstarch and stir well with a wooden spoon. Add the milk, a little at a time, stirring continuously to avoid lumps.
- Switch to a whisk and continue to stir over medium heat until the sauce begins to thicken. The whisk will help to eradicate any lumps. Add more milk as necessary to get the desired thickness. The sauce should have the consistency of custard or pudding.
- Add the cheese and mustard, and stir well. Season with black pepper to taste.
- Drain the macaroni and combine it with the bacon, leek, and cheese sauce. Season to taste and pour into an ovenproof dish, first making sure that it fits well in your halogen.
- Preheat your halogen oven by using the preheat setting or set at 425°F.
- Combine the bread crumbs, oats, and Parmesan cheese and sprinkle over the bake.
- Place on the low rack and cook for 15 minutes until golden and bubbling.

Beef Stroganoff

You could cook this on a stove top in a skillet or frying pan, but I've included this recipe to show you just how versatile your halogen oven is.

- Put a splash of olive oil in a nonstick dish and place this on the high rack. Set the temperature to 425°F.
- Put the beef, onions, and garlic in the dish and cook for 3–6 minutes, turning occasionally.
- Add the mushrooms and butter and cook for another 3–6 minutes, until the mushrooms are tender but not too soft and the onion and beef are cooked.
- Add the herbs, sour cream, and milk, and season to taste. Cover securely with aluminum foil. Place on the low rack and cook for another 8–10 minutes until the sauce is heated.
- Remove the foil, stir well and serve on a bed of pasta or rice.

Splash of olive oil
1 lb 2 oz tenderloin steak, cut into very fine strips
2 onions, finely chopped
1–2 garlic cloves, crushed
$10\frac{1}{2}$ oz or about $3\frac{1}{2}$ cups whole button mushrooms
1 tablespoon butter
2 teaspoons chopped fresh tarragon (or 1 teaspoon of dried)
$1\frac{1}{4}$ cups sour cream
$\frac{1}{2}$ cup plus 2 tablespoons milk
Salt and black pepper, to taste

SERVES 4

4 boneless
   chicken breasts
1 large ball of
   mozzarella, torn
2–3 ripe
   tomatoes, sliced
Handful of fresh
   basil leaves
Salt and black pepper,
   to taste
4–6 slices of proscuitto
Drizzle of olive oil

Mozzarella and Tomato Chicken

A very simple dish that takes minutes to prepare.

- Preheat the halogen oven using the preheat setting, or set the temperature to 400°F.
- Using a sharp knife, cut a slit in each chicken breast to form a pocket. Stuff the pockets with the tomato slices, crumbled mozzarella, and a few basil leaves. Season to taste.
- Wrap securely with the proscuitto, then place the wrapped chicken breasts, seam-side down, on a greased ovenproof dish. Drizzle with olive oil and season to taste.
- Place on the low rack for 20–30 minutes, until the chicken is cooked.

Sausage Casserole

My Aunt Mabel used to make us a similar dish in the autumn, when we stayed on her farm. This is a really hearty dish, perfect for chilly evenings.

- Preheat the halogen oven using the preheat setting, or set the temperature to 450°F.
- Place the sausages, bacon and sliced onion on the browning tray. Drizzle with olive oil and cook on the high rack until the sausages are browned and the onion softened.
- In a casserole dish, first making sure it fits well in your halogen oven, add the sausages, onions, and all remaining ingredients. Season to taste.
- Cover the casserole dish with its own lid, or make a lid using double-folded aluminum foil, securely fastened.
- Place on the low rack and turn the temperature down to 400°F.
- Cook for 20–30 minutes, until the vegetables are soft.
- Serve with mashed or baked potatoes.

1 lb lean, good-quality link sausages
4–6 strips of bacon, chopped
1 large red or Spanish onion, sliced
Drizzle of olive oil
2 garlic cloves, crushed
2 red bell peppers, finely sliced
1 large sweet potato, diced
1 x 14.5 oz can chopped tomatoes
¾ cup red wine
2 teaspoons paprika
Small handful of chopped fresh parsley
Salt and black pepper, to taste

Cheese, Bacon, Bread-and-butter Savory

SERVES 4

6 slices of stale
bread, buttered
3–6 strips of bacon,
diced or roughly
chopped
1 onion, finely
chopped
1½ cups grated mature
Cheddar cheese
3 eggs
2 cups plus
2 tablespoons
of milk
2 sprigs of fresh
thyme, chopped
Salt and black pepper,
to taste

This is a savory variation of the classic British dish known as bread-and butter pudding.

- Grease an ovenproof dish, first making sure it fits well in your halogen oven.
- Use some of the buttered bread to line the dish carefully. Add the bacon, onion, and cheese between layers of bread, building up the layers until you run out of bread.
- Beat the eggs, add the milk and thyme, and season to taste. Pour this over the bread and leave it to settle for about 20 minutes.
- Preheat your halogen oven using the preheat setting or turn to 350°F.
- Top the bread with some grated cheese and season with black pepper. Place on the low rack and cook for 30–40 minutes, until set.

Roasted Herbed Vegetables and Chicken Breasts

SERVES 4

Another way to make a tasty chicken and vegetable dish.

- Preheat the halogen oven using the preheat setting, or set the temperature to 400°F.
- Place the potatoes, sweet potato, and parsnip in a large bowl. Add the paprika and olive oil and combine until well coated.
- Pour this into an ovenproof dish. Add more oil if necessary. Cook for 15 minutes.
- Finely chop the herbs (you can use an electric chopper for this), retaining a small amount for the next step. Add the crushed garlic, 1–2 tablespoons of olive oil and the zest of 1 lemon. mix well.
- Rub half of this mixture over the chicken breasts. Add the chicken to the potatoes and cook for another 15 minutes before adding all remaining ingredients. Sprinkle the remaining herbs over the whole dish and mix well. Add more oil if necessary.
- Bake for another 20–30 minutes, or until the vegetables and chicken are cooked.

1¼ lb new
  potatoes, washed
1 large sweet
  potato, cubed
1 parsnip, quartered
  lengthwise
2 teaspoons paprika
Olive oil
Large handful of fresh
  mixed herbs (such
  as thyme, rosemary,
  oregano)
3–4 garlic
  cloves, crushed
Zest of 1 lemon
1 red or Spanish
  onion, quartered
2–3 baby leeks, cut
  into 3 pieces
4–6 chicken breasts
1–2 red bell peppers,
  thickly sliced
8–12 small vine
  tomatoes, whole

SERVES 4

5 eggs
1 bunch of scallions
    (spring onions),
    finely chopped
1–2 red bell peppers,
    diced or thinly sliced
6 strips of bacon, diced
3–4 sun-dried
    tomatoes, chopped
½ cup grated
    Parmesan
Small handful of fresh
    herbs (basil,
    oregano, or thyme,
    for instance)
Salt and black pepper,
    to taste

Mediterranean-style Tortilla

This is an ideal dish for using up any leftover vegetable.
Anything goes, so experiment!

- Preheat the halogen oven using your preheat setting
  or set the temperature to 400°F.
- Break the eggs into a large bowl and beat well. Add
  all remaining ingredients and stir to combine.
- Pour into a well-greased ovenproof dish. Place on the
  low rack and cook for 20–25 minutes, until firm.
- Serve hot or cold with salad.

Chicken and Bacon Parcels

You can prepare these in advance: they improve with a little marinating. Simply leave in the refrigerator until needed— ideally make them the night before, or in the morning before you leave for work.

- Preheat the halogen oven using the preheat setting, or set the temperature to 400°F.
- Cut 4 double-thickness foil squares, each large enough to hold 1 chicken breast. Grease the middle of each square with oil or butter.
- In a mini chopper or by hand, mix the herbs, garlic, olive oil, and lemon zest together.
- Place a few onion slices on each greased foil parcel.
- Using a teaspoon, smear the herb mixture on the chicken breasts to coat them. Add some mushroom slices and wrap some bacon around each chicken breast. Place the breasts on top of the onion slices in each foil square.
- Add the tablespoon of white wine to each parcel before securing.
- Place the parcels on the low rack and cook for 35–40 minutes, until the chicken is tender.
- Serve with new potatoes and green vegetables.

4 boneless
  chicken breasts
Small handful of fresh
  thyme (or 1–2
  teaspoons of dried)
2–3 garlic
  cloves, crushed
1–2 tablespoons
  olive oil
Zest of 1 lemon
1 small red onion,
  finely sliced
6 mushrooms, sliced
4–6 strips of bacon
4 tablespoons
  white wine
Salt and black pepper,
  to taste

Corned Beef Loaf

4–5 small potatoes,
  cooked and mashed
  (you can use leftover
  mashed potatoes)
1 x 12 oz can corned
  beef, mashed
1 onion, finely
  chopped
2 garlic cloves,
  crushed (optional)
1–2 teaspoons whole-
  grain Dijon mustard
2–3 teaspoons
  tomato paste
1 cup fresh
  wholewheat bread
  crumbs
1 egg, beaten
Salt and black pepper,
  to taste

Here's another easy dish that can be prepared in advance.
Serve it hot or cold.

- Preheat the halogen oven using the preheat setting,
  or set the temperature to 375°F.
- Put the mashed potato and mashed corned beef into
  a very large bowl. Add all the remaining ingredients
  and mix well.
- Pour this into a lined loaf pan, pressing down firmly
  and smoothing out the top.
- Place on the low rack of the halogen oven and bake
  for 25 minutes.
- Leave to cool for 5 minutes before turning out
  into a serving dish. Serve in slices, hot or cold.

Hot Stuffed Chicken with Prosciutto

A simple dish that packs a punch. Enjoy it with new potatoes and green vegetables.

- In a bowl, mix the cream cheese, lemon zest, chili, garlic, and chopped tomato together. Add the cayenne pepper and Tabasco sauce, then add salt and black pepper, to taste.
- Preheat your halogen oven using the preheat setting or set the temperature to 400°F.
- Using a sharp knife, cut a slit in each chicken breast to form a pocket. Use the cream cheese mixture to stuff each chicken breast. Then securely wrap prosciutto around the breast and place it, seam-side down, in an ovenproof dish.
- Drizzle with a little lemon juice and olive oil, and season to taste.
- Place on the low rack and cook for 25–30 minutes until the chicken is cooked.
- Serve with new potatoes and green vegetables.

1 x 8 oz carton of
cream cheese
Zest and juice of
1 lemon
1 chili, finely chopped
2 garlic cloves,
chopped
1 large tomato,
finely chopped
1 pinch of cayenne
pepper to taste
Dash of Tabasco sauce
(optional)
Salt and black pepper,
to taste
4 chicken breasts
4–6 slices of prosciutto
Olive oil

SERVES 4

2 eggplants
A spray of olive oil
1 onion, finely
    chopped
2–3 garlic cloves,
    finely chopped
1 pepper, finely
    chopped (optional)
1¾ cups lean
    ground beef
½ cup red wine
¾ cup mushrooms,
    finely chopped
    (optional)
3–4 fresh tomatoes,
    chopped, or
    1 x 14.5 oz can
    chopped tomatoes
Mixed herbs to taste
Salt and black pepper,
    to taste
Grated cheese, to
    garnish

Stuffed Eggplant

Double this recipe and you can add it later to baked potatoes,
or lasagne.

- Preheat the halogen oven using the preheat setting,
  or set the temperature to 350°F.
- Cut the eggplants in half lengthwise. Using a sharp
  knife, crisscross the middle of each eggplant, leaving
  about 1/3 inch of eggplant flesh along the interior
  walls, then scoop out the rest of the flesh in chunks.
- Brush or spray a small amount of olive oil into each
  eggplant shell. Place the halves on a baking sheet.
- In a skillet or frying pan, fry the onion and garlic in
  a little olive oil until soft and translucent. Add the
  pepper if using.
- Add the ground beef and cook until brown, followed
  by the wine and mushrooms (if using). Cook for
  2 more minutes.
- Add the canned or fresh tomatoes, stirring
  well. Finally, add the herbs and season to taste.
  Simmer for 5 minutes.
- Spoon the sauce into the eggplant half-shells.
- Sprinkle on grated cheese and season to taste.
- Place on the low rack in the halogen oven and cook
  for 30 minutes until the eggplants are soft.
- Serve with salad.

Lamb Shanks

This slow-cook recipe leaves the lamb perfectly tender.
You can speed things up if you want to, but you risk tougher
lamb if you do.

- Put the lamb shanks in a large freezer bag.
- In a bowl, combine the garlic, tomato paste, orange
  zest and juice, red wine, balsamic vinegar, rosemary,
  thyme, and paprika. Season to taste.
- Pour this mixture into the freezer bag with the
  lamb shanks. Shake well to ensure the lamb is
  completely covered. Leave in the refrigerator
  overnight to marinate.
- When ready to cook, preheat the halogen oven using
  the preheat setting, or set the temperature to 325°F.
- Remove the lamb shanks from the freezer bag and
  place them in roasting pan, first making sure the pan
  fits well in your halogen oven.
- Add all the remaining ingredients. Cover with a
  double layer of aluminum foil and secure well.
- Place this on the low rack and cook for 1/4–2 hours.
  You could add some mini baked potatoes (choose a
  recipe from Chapter 3) during the cooking time to
  accompany the dish.
- Remove the foil and cook for another 20–30 minutes
  until the lamb is tender and the sauce has thickened.

4 x 1-lb lamb shanks
3 garlic cloves,
   crushed
3 tablespoons sun-
   dried tomato paste
Zest and juice of
   2 oranges
1¼ cups red wine
3 teaspoons
   balsamic vinegar
2–3 sprigs fresh thyme
2–3 sprigs
   fresh rosemary
2 teaspoons paprika
Salt and black pepper,
   to taste
2 red onions, cut into
   small wedges
2 celery stalks,
   finely sliced
1 leek, finely sliced
1 carrot, finely diced
1 pepper, sliced
1 x 14.5 oz chopped
   tomatoes
1¼ cups lamb or
   beef stock
1 bay leaf

Pea and Ham Soup

SERVES 4

1 red or Spanish
   onion, finely
   chopped
2 tablespoons butter
3 teaspoons of olive oil
1 cup chopped
   cooked ham
1⅓ cups frozen peas
2 sticks of finely
   chopped celery
2 cups hot
   vegetable stock
1¼ cups milk
8 fresh mint leaves
2 tablespoons
   sour cream
Salt and black pepper,
   to taste

- Preheat the halogen oven to 400°F.
- Remove the frozen peas from the freezer so that they start to defrost at room temperature.
- Put the chopped onion, butter, and olive oil in a small casserole dish and cook on the low rack for 8–10 minutes, until the onion starts to soften. (The olive oil helps prevent the butter from burning). Make sure the casserole dish leaves plenty of room for the air to circulate.
- Add the ham and cook for another 3–5 minutes.
- Add the hot stock, milk, frozen peas, finely chopped celery, mint leaves, and seasoning. Cover and cook for another 20–25 minutes.
- Carefully remove the casserole dish from the halogen oven. Add the sour cream and blend the soup using an electric hand/stick blender. Season to taste before servng.

Cheater's Chicken Tikka

SERVES 4

A really simple way to cook chicken tikka. I use Greek yogurt because it holds better than natural yogurt. Serve on a bed of rice with some extra sauce for dressing.

- In a bowl, thoroughly combine the yogurt, onion, garlic, and tikka paste. Add the chili if you like it hot.
- Add the chicken breasts to the bowl and cover them well with the tikka sauce. Cover the bowl with plastic wrap and place it in the refrigerator to marinate overnight, or for at least 1 hour.
- When you're ready to cook, turn the halogen oven to high, as you're going to broil the chicken.
- Place the chicken on the grill pan or browning tray and broil for 8–10 minutes on each side, adding more sauce if and when needed.
- Serve on a bed of rice. Reheat any leftover sauce and pour it over the chicken prior to serving.

14 oz or about 1¾
   cups Greek yogurt
½ onion, very finely
   chopped
2 garlic cloves, finely
   chopped
1 chili, finely chopped
   (optional)
3 tablespoons tikka
   masala curry paste
4 boneless
   chicken breasts

1 tablespoon all-
   purpose flour
3 teaspoons paprika
1 lb 2 oz lean beef
   steak, cut into
   chunks
Drizzle of olive oil
2 red or Spanish
   onions, cut
   into wedges
2–3 garlic cloves,
   finely chopped
2 red bell peppers,
   thickly sliced
1 cup pancetta or
   bacon, diced
10½ oz (about 15–20)
   cherry tomatoes
1 eggplant, diced
1¼ cups red wine
1¼ cups beef stock
2 tablespoons sun-
   dried tomato paste
Small handful of
   fresh thyme and
   oregano, combined
¼ lb pitted
   black olives
Salt and black pepper,
   to taste

Italian Beef Casserole

A very filling dish that is surprisingly simple to prepare.

- Preheat the halogen oven using the preheat setting, or set the temperature to 425°F.
- Put the flour and paprika in a bowl. Add the beef chunks and ensure they're evenly coated with flour.
- Drizzle a little oil into a roasting pan and put it into the halogen oven to heat on the high rack. Once heated, add the beef, onions, and garlic. Return it to the halogen and cook for 5–10 minutes until browned and softened. You may need to stir it a few times during cooking to ensure the meat browns evenly.
- Remove the roasting pan from the oven and add the peppers, pancetta, and cherry tomatoes. Cook again for another 5–8 minutes, stirring occasionally.
- Remove again and add all the remaining ingredients but only half of the fresh herbs. mix well and season to taste. Cover with a double layer of aluminum foil, making sure it is securely fastened.
- Place the dish on the low rack and turn the heat down to 325°F. Cook for 1 hour. Remove the foil and add the remaining herbs. Cook again without the foil for another 10 minutes.
- Serve with baked potatoes.

Ham, Sausage, and Mushroom Ribbons

A tasty pasta dish. You can use spaghetti or tagliatelle.

- Preheat the halogen oven using the preheat setting, or set the temperature to 400°F.
- Prepare the onion, garlic, and sausages while the oven is heating up. Once the oven is preheated, put them in an ovenproof dish with the olive oil and butter.
- Place this dish on the low rack and cook until the sausage slices start to brown and the onions start to soften. You will need to stir or turn them occasionally.
- Meanwhile, place the pasta in a pan of boiling water and cook according to the instructions on the package.
- Add the button mushrooms to the dish and cook until they start to soften.
- While that is cooking, combine the milk, yogurt, and mustard. Season to taste and add half the parsley.
- When the mushrooms and pasta are cooked, drain the pasta and add all the ingredients to the ovenproof dish, including the chopped ham. Place it back in the oven for 5–10 minutes just to heat through.
- Serve with the remaining parsley to garnish.

1 onion, finely chopped
2 garlic cloves
3–4 link sausages, sliced
Drizzle of olive oil
1 tablespoon butter
¾—1 lb spaghetti or tagliatelle pasta
¾ lb or about 3 cups whole button mushrooms
½ cup plus 2 tablespoons milk
¾ cup Greek yogurt
1–2 teaspoons whole-grain Dijon mustard,
Salt and black pepper, to taste
1 small handful chopped parsley
1 cup thick-cut ham chunks

For the tomato sauce
1 onion,
   finely chopped
2–3 garlic cloves,
   finely chopped
A spray of olive oil
1 bell pepper, finely
   chopped (optional)
1¾ cups
   ground turkey
½ cup plus 2
   tablespoons red wine
¾ cup finely chopped
   mushrooms,
   (optional)
3–4 fresh tomatoes,
   chopped, or 1 x
   14.5 oz can
   chopped tomatoes
Mixed herbs to taste
Salt and black pepper,
   to taste

Turkey Lasagne

Why stick to red meat in your lasagne? Ground turkey is tasty and very versatile.

- Fry the onion and garlic in a little olive oil until soft and translucent. Add the pepper at this point if you are including it.
- Add the ground turkey and cook until brown, followed by the wine and mushrooms (if using them), and cook for 2 more minutes.
- Add the canned or fresh tomatoes, stirring well. Finally, add the herbs and season to taste. Leave to simmer for 5 minutes.
- While the tomato sauce is simmering, make the white sauce. Melt the butter gently in a saucepan on medium heat. Add the flour or cornstarch and stir well with a wooden spoon. Add the milk, a little at a time, stirring continuously to avoid lumps.
- Switch now to a whisk. Continue to stir over medium heat until the sauce begins to thicken. The whisk will help to eradicate any lumps. Add more milk as necessary to get the desired thickness. The sauce should have the consistency of custard or pudding. Add the mustard and season with black pepper.
- Preheat the halogen oven using the preheat setting, or set the temperature to 400°F.

- Spoon a layer of tomato sauce mix into the bottom of your lasagne dish, first making sure it fits into the halogen oven, and then pour in a thin layer of white sauce, followed by a layer of lasagne sheets. Continue alternating the layers, finishing with the white sauce. Don't overfill the dish; otherwise the lasagne may spill out during cooking.
- Sprinkle grated cheese over the top.
- Place on the low rack in the halogen oven and cook at 400°F for 40–50 minutes, or until golden and the lasagne sheets are cooked. If the top starts to get too dark, cover it with aluminum foil, making sure it is secure. (The cooking time can be greatly reduced if you use fresh lasagne sheets.)
- Serve with salad and garlic bread.

For the white sauce
2 tablespoons butter
1 tablespoon
  all-purpose flour
  or cornstarch
2–3 cups milk
¼ teaspoon mustard
  (optional)
Black pepper to taste

Sheets of lasagne
  (ensure the
  packagesays "no
  precooking
  required")
Grated cheese,
  to garnish

4 pork chops
¾ cup of
   cream cheese
4–6 teaspoons of pesto
1½ cups fresh
   wholewheat bread
   crumbs
⅓ cup Parmesan
   cheese, grated
Salt and black pepper,
   to taste

Pesto Pork

Perfect for the halogen oven—quick, simple and it tastes great.
Serve with a selection of roasted vegetables.

- Preheat the halogen oven using the preheat setting,
  or set the temperature to 450°F.
- Place the chops or steaks on the grill pan and put it
  on the high rack. Grill for 3–4 minutes each side,
  until they are almost cooked. Remove and set aside.
- Mix the cream cheese and the pesto together.
- In another bowl, mix the bread crumbs and
  Parmesan together and season to taste.
- Pour the pesto mix on the pork, ensuring the tops of
  the chops are covered. Sprinkle with the breadcrumb
  mixture to finish.
- Place the pan back in the halogen on the high rack
  and cook until the topping is golden and bubbling.
  This should take no more than 5 minutes.

Sausage and Mashed Potato Pie

This recipe turns a classic British dish into a delicious one-pot. meal. Vegetarians can make it with vegetarian sausages.

- Preheat the halogen oven using the preheat setting, or set the temperature to 400°F.
- Put the potato, carrot, and sweet potato in a steamer and cook until soft and ready to mash.
- Meanwhile, pour a drizzle of oil in the bottom of an ovenproof dish. Add the sausages, onions, garlic, and red currant jelly. mix well, ensuring that the jelly is mixed in thoroughly.
- Place on the low rack and cook for 20 minutes. Stir with a wooden spoon a couple of times during cooking to combine the flavors again.
- When the sausages have cooked and are browned, cut them into generous bite-size chunks. Add the wine and stock or gravy. Stir well. Put back in the oven and cook for another 10 minutes.
- If you need to thicken the dish, mix the cornstarch with a little water and pour into the gravy, stirring well until thoroughly combined.
- Mash the potatoes and vegetables, adding a little butter or milk if needed.
- Remove the sausage mixture from the oven and spoon the mashed vegetables on top. Return the dish to the oven to brown for 10 minutes.
- Serve with green vegetables.

4–5 potatoes, diced
2 carrots, diced
1 sweet potato, diced
Drizzle of olive oil
6–8 good-quality
  link sausages
1–2 red onions, sliced
1 clove of garlic,
  crushed
1 tablespoon
  red currant jelly
½ cup red wine
¾–1¼ cups gravy
  or hot stock
1 teaspoon cornstarch
  (optional)
2 tablespoons butter
  or ¼ cup milk
Salt and black pepper,
  to taste

Fish

As a nutritionist, I strongly recommend that you eat fish—preferably oily, sustainable, omega-rich fish—at least two or three times a week. Always buy fresh whenever you can.

This chapter contains plenty of ideas to help inspire you. Some people say that you should never mix cheese and fish, but I disagree—so you'll find some recipes including both these ingredients in the following pages.

CHAPTER

5

Roasted Fish with Fennel and Onion

SERVES 4

2–4 white fish fillets

Salt and black pepper, to taste

2 lemons (1 cut into wedges)

1 large or 2 small fennel bulbs, sliced

2 red or Spanish onions, sliced

2–3 garlic cloves, finely sliced

Drizzle of olive oil

2 tablespoons butter

- Preheat the halogen oven using the preheat setting, or set the temperature to 425°F.
- Prepare the fish fillets, season well, and squeeze a little fresh lemon juice over them. Set the fish aside.
- Place the sliced fennel, onion, garlic, and lemon wedges in a roasting pan, first making sure the tray fits your halogen oven.
- Drizzle with olive oil and put in the oven on the low rack for 15 minutes.
- Put the fish on top of the vegetables and place a small pat of butter on each fillet. Squeeze the juice of the other lemon over the dish. Season to taste.
- Cover securely with aluminum foil. Bake for another 15–20 minutes, until the fish is thoroughly cooked and flakes easily off a fork.
- Remove the foil and serve with new potatoes and a fresh green salad.

Fish Burgers

You can prepare these in advance, or freeze them until needed.

- In a large bowl, thoroughly mix the scalllions, fish, tarragon, and lemon juice. Season before adding the beaten egg. Mix thoroughly.
- Gradually add the bread crumbs and flour until you have a firm but moist mixture.
- Form the mixture into balls—again, these should be firm but moist. Use the palm of your hand to flatten the balls into burger shapes.
- Put the burgers in the refrigerator until ready to use, or freeze them in layers (separate each layer with wax paper to prevent them from sticking).
- To cook, brush the burgers lightly with olive oil. Turn the halogen oven to 475°F. Put the burgers on the high rack and cook for 4–5 minutes on each side until golden.
- Serve with wholewheat buns and a salad garnish, or chunky homemade fries and peas for a variation on the classic British fish and chips.

SERVES 4

½ bunch of scallions (spring onions) finely chopped
½ lb cod fillet, finely chopped
½ lb white fish fillet, finely chopped
1 teaspoon dried tarragon
Juice of ½ lemon
Salt and black pepper, to taste
1 egg, beaten
1 tablespoon fresh wholewheat bread crumbs
1 tablespoon all-purpose flour

SERVES 4

2¼ lb potatoes
1 lb fish fillets (or
   pieces of flaky
   white fish)
½ lb salmon pieces
   (optional)
¼ lb shrimp
   (optional)
1 cup of milk
2 tablespoons butter
¼ cup all-purpose
   flour
1 teaspoon dry
   mustard
Salt and black pepper,
   to taste
A little grated cheese,
   for topping

Creamy Fish Pie

This is a real family favorite and it'sperfect for the halogen oven. You can also prepare this pie in advance.

- Boil or steam the potatoes until tender, then mash them with a little butter and set aside.
- Meanwhile, put the fish and milk in a pan and bring the milk to scalding point. Reduce the heat and simmer for 10 minutes, or until the fish is cooked through.
- Drain the fish and reserve the liquid for making the sauce. Shred the fish and put it in a pie plate.
- To make a creamy sauce, melt the butter in a pan and add the flour. Stir in the reserved milk stock and heat gently until the sauce thickens. I normally use a whisk at this stage to prevent lumps from forming. Stir continuously. Add the mustard and season to taste.
- Pour the sauce over the fish.
- Preheat the halogen oven using the preheat setting, or set the temperature to 400°F.
- Cover the fish with the mashed potatoes and top with a small amount of grated cheese.
- Place in the halogen on the low rack. Bake for 20–25 minutes, or until golden on top.

Salmon, Sweet Potato, and Chili Fish Cakes

These fishcakes are packed with goodness: omega oil-rich salmon and antioxidant-rich sweet potato.

- Combine the bread crumbs and farina, season, and set aside.
- In a bowl mix the fish, sweet potatoes, scallions, chilies, cumin, lemon juice, and cilantro. Add a little beaten egg to bind if necessary. Season to taste.
- Form the mixture into cakes—if it's too wet, add a little all-purpose flour. Once the cakes are formed, you can leave them to rest or continue with the coating.
- To coat the fish cakes, brush each one with a little beaten egg, then dip it into the breadcrumb mixture. This is a little messy, so be prepared! Put the cakes on wax paper and chill in the refrigerator for 10 minutes.
- Preheat the halogen oven using the preheat setting, or set the temperature to 475°F.
- Remove the fish cakes from the refrigerator and brush with a light coating of olive oil, but be careful not to displace the topping.
- Place the fish cakes on the high rack, either on a baking sheet or browning pan, or you can place them directly on the rack.
- Cook for 5–6 minutes on each side, turning to ensure they are evenly browned.
- Serve with a fresh green salad and new potatoes.

SERVES 4

1 cup fresh wholewheat bread crumbs
2 tablespoons farina
Salt and black pepper, to taste
2 x 6-oz cans salmon
¾ lb sweet potatoes, cooked and mashed
3 scallions (spring onions), finely chopped
2 chilies, finely chopped
1 teaspoon ground cumin
1 tablespoon lemon juice
Small handful of fresh cilantro, finely chopped
2 eggs, beaten
Olive oil

Italian Fish

4 fish fillets
  (cod is fine)
Drizzle of lemon juice
4–6 strips of bacon
1 ball of mozzarella
4–8 sun-dried
  tomatoes
Small handful of fresh
  basil leaves
Salt and black pepper,
  to taste
Drizzle of olive oil

- Turn the halogen oven to high (for broiling).
- Place the fish fillets on a broiling pan and drizzle with a little lemon juice and olive oil. Broil for 2 minutes on the high rack.
- Turn the fillets over and add the bacon to the pan beside (not on top) of the fish. Broil for another 2 minutes, then remove from the oven.
- Layer the bacon, mozzarella, basil leaves, and sun-dried tomatoes on the fish. Season to taste and drizzle with a little olive oil.
- Put back in the halogen for another 3–4 minutes.

Simple Baked Trout

- Preheat the halogen oven using the preheat setting, or set the temperature to 400°F.
- Mix the butter and herbs together in a bowl to form a herb butter.
- Cut a piece of foil to almost double the size of each trout and butter it with the herb butter. Place each trout on the foil and drizzle lemon juice over it.
- Stuff each fish with herb butter and a slice or two of lemon. Add a tablespoon of water to each fish. Drizzle with olive oil and season with black pepper.
- Seal the foil securely and place on a baking sheet or directly on the low rack. Cook for 20–30 minutes until the fish is tender and flaking.
- Serve with new potatoes and green vegetables.

2–3 tablespoons butter
Small handful of fresh
  herbs (rosemary,
  sweet marjoram or
  dill, or a mixture),
  finely chopped
4 whole trout, about
  12 oz each, cleaned
  and boned
1 lemon, sliced
4 tablespoons water
Drizzle of olive oil
Black pepper to taste

Cod, Egg, and Gruyère Bake

SERVES 4

1 lb cod fillets,
  roughly chopped
2–3 hard-boiled eggs,
  halved or quartered
1 cup crème fraîche or
  sour cream
½ cup plus 2
  tablespoons milk
1¼ cups grated
  Gruyère cheese
2 teaspoons whole-
  grain Dijon mustard,
Salt and black pepper,
  to taste
2 tablespoons
  bread crumbs
1 tablespoon
  rolled oats
½ cup grated
  Parmesan cheese

This is such a quick and easy dish and it's perfect as a warming supper.

- Preheat the halogen oven using the preheat settings, or turn it on to 350°F.
- Put the chopped cod and hard-boiled eggs in an ovenproof dish.
- In a bowl, mix the crème fraîche, milk, grated cheese, and mustard. Season to taste. Spoon this over the egg and cod mixture.
- Mix the bread crumbs, oats, and Parmesan. Season well and sprinkle on top of the crème fraîche mixture.
- Place on the low rack and bake in the oven for 15–20 minutes, until the cod is cooked.

Tuna and Corn Lasagne

Tuna and corn really work well together. If you want to speed up the cooking time, boil the lasagne sheets for 8–10 minutes before adding them—this should knock off about 15 minutes. Alternatively, use fresh pasta sheets, but these are usually more expensive.

- Mix the tuna, scallions, and corn together in a bowl. Season to taste.
- Add a layer of this tuna mixture to the bottom of a lasagne dish, cover with a layer of lasagne sheets, and top with a layer of passata. Repeat this process, ending with a layer of passata.
- Preheat the halogen oven using the preheat setting, or set the temperature to 400°F.
- Grate Parmesan over the top of the dish and sprinkle with black pepper.
- Place on the low rack and cook for 40–50 minutes (30 minutes if using pre-boiled or fresh pasta sheets) until golden and the lasagne sheets are cooked. If the top starts to get too dark, cover with aluminum foil, making sure it is secure.
- Serve with salad and garlic bread.

1 x 12 oz tuna, mashed
3–4 scallions (spring onions), chopped
1 generous cup corn (canned or frozen)
Salt and black pepper, to taste
Lasagne sheets
2 cups passata (tomato purée)
Grated Parmesan or other mature hard cheese, for topping

Baked Sea Bass with Red Pesto

4 sea bass fillets
4 slices of lemon
4 teaspoons of
  red pesto
1 red or Spanish
  onion, sliced
Olive oil
1–2 tablespoons
  white wine
Salt and black pepper,
  to taste

- Preheat the halogen oven using the preheat setting, or turn on to 400°F.
- Cut out four squares of aluminum foil, twice the size of each fillet. Grease each one with a little butter.
- Place one slice of lemon in the middle of each square. Place a fillet on top of it. Add 1 teaspoon of red pesto to each fillet. Cover with some onion slices.
- Drizzle with olive oil and white wine. Season well and secure the foil into a parcel.
- Place on the low rack and cook for 20–25 minutes, until the fish is cooked and flaky.

Tomato and Tuna Gratin

- Preheat the halogen oven using the preheat setting, or set the temperature to 400°F.
- Chop the tuna into chunks and put in an ovenproof dish.
- Heat the olive oil in a skillet or frying pan. Add the onions, garlic, and red pepper and cook until they start to soften. Add the chopped tomatoes, a splash of balsamic vinegar, and the herbs. Season to taste. Pour this over the tuna.
- In a bowl, mix the bread crumbs, oats, and grated cheese and season to taste. Sprinkle this mixture over the tomato mixture.
- Place in the oven on the low rack and cook for 15 minutes.

1 x 12 oz can tuna
Drizzle of olive oil
1 red or Spanish
  onion, finely
  chopped
2 garlic cloves,
  crushed
½ red pepper, diced
1 x 14.5 oz can
  chopped tomatoes
Balsamic vinegar
Small handful of fresh
  basil, chopped
½ teaspoon
  dried thyme
Salt and black pepper,
  to taste
1½ cups fresh
  wholewheat
  bread crumbs
½ cup rolled oats
½ cup grated mature
  Cheddar cheese

Red Snapper and Tomato Bake

1 lb 2 oz red
snapper fillets

Salt and black pepper,
to taste

Drizzle of olive oil

2 garlic cloves,
crushed

1 red or Spanish
onion, finely
chopped

½ cup sun-dried
tomatoes, chopped

3 ripe vine tomatoes

1 cup red wine

Handful of fresh
basil, chopped

- Preheat the halogen oven using the preheat setting, or turn the temperature to 375°F.
- Put the fish fillets in an ovenproof dish. Season to taste.
- In a skillet or frying pan, add the oil, garlic, and onions. Fry until the onion starts to become translucent. (If you prefer, cook the onions and garlic in the halogen by putting them on the high rack and cooking on high heat until translucent. Add this to the fish, then add the remaining ingredients. Add the basil once you've removed the dish from the halogen.)
- Add the tomatoes, wine, and most of the basil to the pan. Cook for another 2–3 minutes. Remove and pour the contents over the fish.
- Cover the dish with aluminum foil. Bake on the low rack for 20 minutes, or until the fish is cooked.
- Garnish with the remaining basil to serve.

Baked Flounder with Cherry Tomato and Basil Drizzle

SERVES 4

- Preheat the halogen oven using the preheat setting, or set to 400°F.
- Put the new potatoes, paprika, mixed herbs, and a drizzle of olive oil in a bowl. Mix well. Transfer to a baking sheet and put on the low rack for 25 minutes.
- In a small baking dish, combine the cherry tomatoes, garlic, half the basil, and a drizzle of olive oil. Season with the sugar, a sprinkle of salt, and some black pepper. Mix well, cover with aluminum foil and set aside.
- Season the fish and drizzle with lemon juice. Place the fish over the almost-cooked new potatoes.
- Put the tomato and basil mixture on the high rack above the fish and cook for 10–15 minutes, until the fish and the potatoes are cooked.
- To serve, put potatoes and fish on each plate. Stir the remaining fresh basil into the tomato and basil mixture and drizzle it on top. Serve with steamed green vegetables.

$2\frac{1}{4}$ lb new potatoes, washed
2 teaspoons paprika
1 teaspoon mixed dried herbs
Olive oil
$\frac{1}{2}$ lb cherry tomatoes, halved
2–3 garlic cloves, finely sliced
Small handful of fresh basil
1 teaspoon sugar
Salt and black pepper, to taste
4 small pieces of flounder, cleaned and boned
Drizzle of lemon juice

Baked Herb Salmon

SERVES 4

Handful of fresh basil

Small handful of
    fresh dill

Juice of 2 lemons

2–3 tablespoons
    olive oil

1 red onion, sliced

1 whole salmon,
    cleaned, boned
    and ready to cook

- Preheat the halogen oven using the preheat setting, or set the temperature to 400°F.
- Put the herbs, lemon juice, and olive oil in a food processor and blitz until combined.
- Cut a piece of aluminum foil large enough to parcel the salmon. Butter the foil and add the sliced onions. Place the salmon on top of the onions.
- Stuff the salmon with half of the herb paste and use the remainder to cover it.
- Fold the foil around the fish in a parcel, making sure the edges are sealed well.
- Place on the low rack and cook for 25–35 minutes, depending on the size of the fish, until it flakes easily.
- Serve with new potatoes and green vegetables.

Creamy Baked Cod

- Preheat the halogen oven using the preheat setting, or set the temperature to 350°F.
- Butter the base of an ovenproof dish, first making sure it fits your halogen oven.
- Butter and season the fillets, then roughly chop them. Place them in the ovenproof dish and add the sliced onion.
- In a bowl, mix the lemon zest and juice, mustard, crème fraîche, milk, and parsley, and season with black pepper. Mix well.
- Pour this over the fish and spread evenly. Sprinkle with grated Parmesan and black pepper.
- Place on the low rack and cook for 25–30 minutes, until the fish is tender.

1¾ lb cod fillets
1 red or Spanish onion, sliced
2½ tablespoons butter
Salt and black pepper, to taste
Juice and zest of 1 lemon
2 teaspoons whole-grain Dijon mustard
½ cup plus 2 tablespoons crème fraîche or sour cream
½ cup plus 2 tablespoons milk
Small handful fresh parsley, chopped
Black pepper
Parmesan cheese, grated

SERVES 4

Juice of ½ lemon
4 salmon fillets
1–2 tablespoons
   whole-grain Dijon
   mustard
1–2 tablespoons honey
2 tablespoons
   wholewheat
   bread crumbs
1 tablespoon
   cornflakes, crushed
   (if you don't have
   cornflakes, use finely
   chopped nuts)

Honey-Mustard Salmon

Simple yet delicious.

- Preheat the halogen oven using the preheat setting, or set the temperature to 400°F.
- Squeeze the lemon juice over the salmon fillets.
- Mix the mustard and honey together. In another bowl, mix the bread crumbs and cornflakes together.
- Spread the mustard-honey mixture on the fillets, ensuring they're well coated. Dip the fish into the bread crumbs—again, ensuring they're well coated.
- Put the fillets on a baking sheet and place on the low rack. Cook for 12–15 minutes, until they are done.
- Serve with a green salad and new potatoes.

Stuffed Trout

- Preheat the halogen oven using the preheat setting, or set the temperature to 375°F.
- Put the trout in an ovenproof dish. Squeeze lemon juice over it and season.
- In a skillet or frying pan, sauté the onion and bacon in a little olive oil. (You can do this in the halogen if you prefer, on the high rack using high heat— remember to turn the temperature back down afterwards.) Once cooked, remove and place in a mixing bowl.
- Add the bread crumbs, zest and remaining lemon juice, parsley, and cream cheese. Mix thoroughly, then use this mixture to stuff the trout.
- Cover with foil and place on the low rack of the halogen. Cook for 20 minutes, or until the trout flesh flakes easily.
- Serve with new potatoes and green vegetables.

1 large whole trout, cleaned and boned
Juice and zest of 1 lemon
Salt and black pepper, to taste
Drizzle of olive oil
1 small onion, finely chopped
3–4 strips of bacon, chopped
1½ cups fresh wholewheat bread crumbs
Small handful of fresh parsley, chopped
8 oz or 1 cup cream cheese

Tomato, Shrimp, and Fish Stew

SERVES 4–6

Drizzle of olive oil
1 onion, finely
  chopped
2 garlic cloves,
  crushed
1 red bell pepper,
  deseeded and diced
1 x 14.5 oz can
  chopped tomatoes,
  or 6 ripe tomatoes
1¼ cups warm
  fish stock
1¼ cups white wine
1¼ lb fish fillets
  or pieces
A dozen shrimp
2 bay leaves
Handful of fresh
  parsley, chopped
Salt and black pepper,
  to taste

- Heat the oil in a skillet or frying pan and fry the onions, garlic, and pepper for 2–3 minutes.
- Preheat the halogen using the preheat setting, or set the temperature to 350°F.
- Place the onion mixture and all remaining ingredients into an ovenproof casserole dish and mix well. Season to taste.
- Cover with the casserole lid or use a piece of aluminum foil, secured well.
- Place on the low rack and cook for 40 minutes before serving.

Red Snapper with Mushroom and Cashew Stuffing

SERVES 4

- Preheat the halogen oven using the preheat setting, or set the temperature to 375°F.
- Put the prepared fish on squares of aluminum foil. Squeeze the lemon juice over the fish and season to taste.
- In a skillet or frying pan, sauté the onion in a little olive oil. Add the chopped mushrooms, cashews, and bread crumbs. (I use a food processor to chop all the ingredients finely.) Cook for a couple of minutes before adding the parsley.
- Use this mixture to stuff each fish.
- Add the water and ½ teaspoon of butter to each aluminum foil square. Season to taste before folding the foil around the fish.
- Place on the low rack of the halogen and cook for 20 minutes, or until the fish is flaking.
- Serve with new potatoes and green vegetables.

4 small red snapper, cleaned, boned and ready to stuff
Juice of 1 lemon
Salt and black pepper, to taste
Drizzle of olive oil
1 small onion, finely chopped
1 cup mushrooms, finely chopped
¾ cup cashews, finely chopped
1 scant cup fresh wholewheat bread crumbs
Small handful of fresh parsley, chopped
4 tablespoons water
2 teaspoons butter

Salmon Fish Cakes

SERVES 4

1 x 14–15 oz
    can salmon
1 lb potatoes, cooked
    and mashed
2 teaspoons
    lemon juice
1–2 teaspoons
    fresh dill (or 1
    teaspoon dried)
1–2 teaspoons fresh
    tarragon (or 1
    teaspoon dried)
2 eggs, beaten
Drizzle of olive oil
All-purpose flour,
    for rolling

• Mix the fish, potatoes, lemon juice, and herbs together in a bowl. Add the egg to bind.

• Form the mixture into cakes. If they are too wet, roll them in a little all-purpose flour, but dust off to remove any excess. Put the cakes on wax paper and chill in the refrigerator for 10 minutes.

• Preheat the halogen oven using the preheat setting, or set the temperature to 475°F.

• Remove the cakes from the refrigerator and brush them with a light coating of olive oil. Put them on the high rack, either on a baking sheet or browning pan or directly on the rack itself.

• the cakes for 5–6 minutes each side, ensuring that both sides are evenly cooked and browned. (You are actually grilling them at this heat!)

Cod and Cheese Gratin

- Preheat the halogen oven using the preheat setting, or set the temperature to 350°F.
- Mix the crème fraîche, parsley, mustard, and mature cheese in a bowl. Season to taste.
- Put the fish pieces in the bottom of an ovenproof dish. Pour the crème fraîche mixture over the fish.
- Mix the oats, bread crumbs, and Parmesan. Season and sprinkle on top of the crème fraîche mixture.
- Place on the low rack and cook for 15–20 minutes.

SERVES 4

1 cup crème fraîche or sour cream
Small handful of fresh parsley, chopped
1 teaspoon whole-grain Dijon mustard, such as Dijon country-style
1 cup mature grated cheese, such as Cheddar
Salt and black pepper, to taste
3–4 skinless cod fillets, roughly chopped
1 cup rolled oats
2 cups fresh wholewheat bread crumbs
½ cup grated Parmesan

Italian-style Cod

SERVES 4

4 cod fillets
1–2 tablespoons pesto
1 red or Spanish
 onion, sliced
 into rings
6–8 sprigs of
 fresh thyme
4 strips of bacon
Dash of olive oil
Black pepper

- Preheat the halogen oven using the preheat setting, or set the temperature to 425°F.
- Cover each fillet with a layer of pesto and add some onion rings and fresh thyme. Wrap a strip of pancetta around each fillet and place it on a square of greased baking parchment or foil, large enough to package the fillet securely. Drizzle with olive oil and season with black pepper.
- Seal the parcels and place them on a baking sheet or directly on the low rack. Cook for 15–20 minutes, until the fish is tender and flaky.
- Serve with new potatoes and green vegetables.

Breaded Salmon Fillets

SERVES 4

This is so simple but tastes divine and looks quite impressive. Serve with green salad and new potatoes.

- Preheat the halogen oven using the preheat setting, or set the temperature to 425°F.
- Place the bread crumbs, oats, chives, parsley, Parmesan, and lemon zest and juice in a bowl and mix well.
- Cover the fillets with cream cheese (or just the tops if you don't want to get too messy!).
- Dip the fillets into the bread-crumb mixture, ensuring they are well covered, and then put them on a greased or lined baking sheet.
- Place on the low rack and bake in the oven for 20 minutes.
- Serve with salad and new potatoes.

1 cup fresh
 wholewheat
 bread crumbs
1 tablespoon
 rolled oats
1 tablespoon chives
1 tablespoon parsley
1 tablespoon grated
 Parmesan cheese
Zest of 1 lemon
Juice of ½ lemon
4 salmon fillets (or any
 other fish fillet)
4–5 teaspoons low-fat
 cream cheese

Herby Salmon Parcels

1–2 tablespoons butter

Small handful of fresh
  herbs (e.g. parsley
  and dill), finely
  chopped

4 salmon fillets

1 lemon, sliced

4 tablespoons water

Olive oil

Black pepper to
  season

- Preheat the halogen oven using the preheat setting, or set the temperature to 425°F.
- Mix the butter and herbs together to form a herb butter.
- Cut 4 squares of aluminum foil, large enough to parcel each fillet.
- Cover each fillet with a layer of herb butter, a slice or two of lemon, and 2 teaspoons of water. Drizzle with olive oil and season with black pepper.
- Seal the parcels and place them on a baking sheet or directly on the low rack. Cook for 15–20 minutes, or until the fish is tender and flaking.
- Serve with new potatoes and green vegetables.

Simple Mackerel Parcels

SERVES 4

- Preheat the halogen oven using the preheat setting, or set the temperature to 400°F.
- Prepare the fish and season well.
- Cut 4 squares of aluminum foil, large enough to parcel each fillet. Grease well.
- Place each fillet in the center of the foil and add 1 teaspoon of butter, 1 lemon slice and 2 teaspoons of water. Season and wrap securely.
- Place the fish parcels on the low rack and cook for 20 minutes.
- Unwrap and serve immediately.

4 Spanish
mackerel fillets
4 teaspoons butter,
plus extra for
greasing
4 slices of lemon
8 teaspoons of water
(2 per piece of fish)
Salt and black pepper,
to taste

6 oz (about 6 cups)
fresh spinach
2–3 cups milk
1 lb cod fillets
1½ tablespoons butter
2 heaped tablespoons
all-purpose flour
1 cup grated
mature Cheddar
1 teaspoon whole-
grain Dijon mustard
Pinch of cayenne
pepper
Salt and black pepper,
to taste

Cod Florentine

- Preheat the halogen oven using the preheat setting, or set the temperature to 400°F.
- Steam the spinach for 5 minutes so that it wilts. Once soft, place it in a greased ovenproof dish and push down to form a base.
- Pour the milk into a saucepan, bring it up to scalding point, then add the cod fillets. Simmer until the cod is cooked (flaking off the fork). Remove the fish (reserving the milk), flake or chop it, and put it onto the bed of spinach.
- Meanwhile, melt the butter in a saucepan. Add the flour to form a paste. Gradually add the hot milk and stir well. Use a whisk to remove any lumps.
- Add almost all the cheese, retaining some for the topping. Add the mustard and cayenne pepper and season to taste. Once the cheese has melted, pour this sauce over the cod mixture.
- Garnish with remaining cheese. Place on the low rack and cook for 10–15 minutes until golden on top.

Salsa Chili Red Snapper

- Preheat the halogen oven using the preheat setting, or set the temperature to 375°F.
- Put the fish in an ovenproof dish. Squeeze the lime juice on top and season to taste.
- Chop and prepare the remaining ingredients. Mix together thoroughly and pour on top of the fillets.
- Cover with aluminum foil and place on the low rack of the halogen. Cook for 20 minutes, or until the fish is flaking.
- Serve with new potatoes and green vegetables.

4 red snapper fillets
Juice of 1 lime
Salt and black pepper,
   to taste
1 tablespoon olive oil
3 ripe tomatoes,
   chopped
1 small red or Spanish
   onion, diced
1 red pepper, diced
1–2 chilies,
   finely chopped
2–3 garlic
   cloves, crushed
Small handful of fresh
   cilantro, chopped
1 cup vermouth

Tomato and Tuna Bake

SERVES 4

Olive oil

2 garlic cloves, crushed

1 red or Spanish onion, finely chopped

4–6 ripe tomatoes, quartered

Sprinkle of sea salt

Sprinkle of sugar

2 teaspoons balsamic vinegar

Handful of chopped fresh basil

10–12 oz (about 3 cups) dried pasta twirls

2 x 5 oz cans tuna, drained and crumbled

½ cup mozzarella

Black pepper, to taste

- Preheat the halogen oven using the preheat setting, or turn the temperature to 350°F.
- Place the oil, garlic, onions, and tomatoes in an ovenproof dish. Sprinkle with sea salt, sugar, and balsamic vinegar. Add half of the fresh basil.
- Place on the low rack and cook for 20–30 minutes. While this is cooking, cook and drain the pasta, following the instructions on the package.
- Remove the tomatoes from the halogen. Add the cooked pasta and crumbled tuna. mix well. Finish with crumbled mozzarella, a drizzle of olive oil and season with black pepper.
- Bake on the low rack for 10–15 minutes at 375°F, then serve immediately.

Smoked Mackerel and Leek Pie

A variation on a family favorite.

- Cut the potato and sweet potato into pieces of an equal size, ready to steam.
- While the potatoes are steaming, fry the leeks in a little butter to soften them.
- Place the softened leeks in a bowl and add the mackerel, crème fraîche, Greek yogurt, Parmesan, and parsley. Mix thoroughly and season to taste. If it looks too dry, add a little milk. Pour this mixture into an ovenproof pie plate.
- Mash the potatoes together with a little butter and season well. Spoon over the mackerel mixture.
- Place on the low rack and cook at 400°F for 20–25 minutes until golden.

SERVES 4

1¼ lb potatoes
¾ lb sweet potatoes
2–3 leeks, diced
Butter for frying and mashing
1 lb smoked mackerel fillets, diced
1 cup crème fraîche or sour cream
½ cup Greek yogurt
½ cup grated Parmesan
Small handful of freshly chopped parsley
Dash of milk (optional)
Salt and black pepper, to taste

SERVES 4

⅓ cup all-purpose
  flour
¾ cup rolled oats
½ cup grated
  Parmesan,
1½ cups fresh
  wholewheat
  bread crumbs
Salt and black pepper,
  to taste
1–2 eggs, beaten
2–4 salmon fillets

Salmon Fish Sticks

This is a really simple idea for the frozen fish sticks kids seem to adore. Use any white fish instead of salmon if you prefer.

- Preheat the halogen oven using the preheat setting, or set the temperature to 400°F.
- In a bowl, mix the flour, oats, Parmesan, and bread crumbs. Season to taste.
- In another bowl, beat the eggs.
- Cut the salmon into thick fingers. Dip each into the egg mixture, then into the breadcrumb mixture, ensuring at each stage that the fish is evenly coated.
- Place on a well-greased baking tray. Cook on the low rack for 15–20 minutes, until crunchy and the salmon is cooked.
- Serve with potato wedges (see Chapter 3).

Individual Cod Puff Pies

Cook these pies in small ramekins. You can also cook it as one large dish, but you may need to adjust the cooking time.

- Preheat the halogen oven using the preheat setting, or set the temperature to 400°F.
- In a bowl, mix the fish with the crème fraîche, milk, and lemon zest and season to taste. Mix well.
- Put this mixture in the ramekin dishes and add the halved soft-boiled egg. Cover with grated cheese.
- Roll out about a quarter of the puff pastry to a $\frac{1}{8}$–$\frac{1}{4}$ inch thickness. Cut out pastry lids to cover the ramekin dishes. To seal the lids you may need to place a small amount of pastry around the edges of each dish to form a lip—something for the pastry to grip onto. Then seal with a little milk or water. Cut a small slit in the top of each pastry lid to allow air to escape. Brush with milk, beaten egg or water.
- Place on the low rack and cook for 20–25 minutes.

SERVES 4–5

1 lb cod, cut into chunks
1 cup crème fraîche or sour cream
$\frac{1}{4}$ cup milk
Zest of 1 lemon
Salt and black pepper, to taste
2–3 soft-boiled eggs, halved
$\frac{1}{3}$–$\frac{1}{2}$ cup grated mature cheese
1 package store-bought puff pastry

Cheesy Pollock Layer

A filling dish with multiple layers of flavor.

4 pollock (or cod)
fillets

Juice and zest of
1 lemon

4 oz or about 3 cups
raw baby leaf
spinach

3 tomatoes, sliced

8 oz (about 1 cup)
crème fraîche or
sour cream

1 cup milk

1 cup grated
Parmesan cheese

1 scant cup fresh
wholewheat
bread crumbs

⅓ cup rolled oats

Salt and black pepper,
to taste

- Preheat the halogen oven using the preheat setting,
  or set the temperature to 400°F.
- Squeeze almost all of the lemon juice over the fillets
  and set aside.
- In the base of an ovenproof dish, place a layer of
  spinach leaves. On top of this, add the tomato slices,
  then season with black pepper.
- Put the fish fillets on top of the tomatoes. Add the
  remaining lemon juice and the zest.
- In a bowl, mix the crème fraîche, milk, and ¾ cup of
  grated Parmesan cheese. Season to taste before
  pouring this mixture over the fish.
- In another bowl, mix the bread crumbs, oats, and
  remaining Parmesan. Mix and season well. Sprinkle
  this over the sauce.
- Place in the oven on the low rack and cook for
  25 minutes until golden.

Mustard Cod

A simple dish with a crispy coating of whole-grain mustard.

- Preheat the halogen oven using the preheat setting, or set the temperature to 400°F.
- Squeeze some lemon juice over the fillets.
- Mix the mustard, bread crumbs, oats, and black pepper together.
- Brush the fillets with olive oil. Spread on the mustard coating, ensuring that the tops of the fillets are well coated.
- Place the fillets on a baking sheet and cook on the low rack for 12–15 minutes, or until the fish is cooked.
- Serve with a green salad and new potatoes.

SERVES 4

Juice of 1 lemon
4 cod fillets
2–3 tablespoons whole-grain Dijon mustard
1½ cups wholewheat bread crumbs
½ cup rolled oats
Black pepper to taste
Drizzle of olive oil

Thai Fish Bakes

SERVES 4

For the sauce
1⅓-inch piece of root
  ginger, finely
  chopped
2–3 chilies, finely
  chopped
1–2 sticks of
  lemongrass,
  finely chopped
Juice and zest of
  1 lime
3–4 lime leaves,
  chopped
4 teaspoons Thai paste
1 x 14 oz can of
  coconut milk
½ cup plus 2
  tablespoons
  Greek yogurt
Salt and black pepper,
  to taste
Small handful of fresh
  cilantro, chopped

4 fish fillets
1½–2 cups cooked
  Thai lime pilaf
  (or plain rice)

You can use whatever fish you prefer in this recipe. Simply prepare the Thai sauce, pour it over the fish, and secure in foil. For added flavor, marinate the fish for an hour or two before baking. You could also use a Thai meal kit, which contains coconut milk, Thai paste, herbs, and spices—cheaper than buying each item individually.

- Prepare the Thai sauce by mixing together the ginger, chilies, lemongrass, lime juice, zest, and leaves, Thai paste, coconut milk, and Greek yogurt. Season to taste before adding half the cilantro.
- Place each fish fillet on a double-layer aluminum foil square, large enough for a portion of rice to be added later and to fold and secure into a parcel.
- Pour the Thai sauce over the fish, dividing it evenly among each portion—if any sauce is left over, reserve it for later. Leave to marinate for at least 1 hour.
- Preheat the halogen oven using the preheat setting, or set the temperature to 350°F.
- Put the parcels on the low rack and cook for 15 minutes.
- Meanwhile, cook the Thai rice according to the package instructions. Undo each parcel and add a portion of rice, along with any remaining sauce, and reseal. Place back in the oven and cook for a further 5–8 minutes.
- To serve, garnish with the remaining cilantro.

Salmon and Cheese Cannelloni

This is such a simple dish to make, but it looks impressive and tastes even better!

- Put the spinach in a colander and run under hot water for a couple of minutes to soften the leaves.
- In a bowl, mix the salmon, ricotta, spinach, lemon zest, dill, and nutmeg.
- Cook the dried lasagne sheets in boiling water for 5–8 minutes, then drain.
- Add the salmon and ricotta mixture to one end of each sheet. Roll up firmly to form cannelloni tubes and place seal-side down in an ovenproof dish in a single layer.
- Preheat the halogen oven using the preheat setting, or set the temperature to 375°F.
- While the oven is preheating, mix the crème fraîche, onions, cheese, and seasoning together and pour this over the cannelloni.
- Sprinkle with a mixture of bread crumbs and Parmesan before placing on the low rack. Cook for 30 minutes, until the cannelloni is cooked.
- Serve with garlic bread and green salad.

1½ cups fresh baby leaf spinach
10 oz salmon fillets, shredded
1 cup of ricotta cheese
Zest of 1 lemon, finely chopped
Small handful of fresh dill, finely chopped
¼ teaspoon grated nutmeg
8 lasagne sheets
1 lb 2 oz crème fraîche or sour cream
1 small red or Spanish onion, finely chopped
¾ cup grated mature Cheddar
Salt and black pepper, to taste
1 cup fresh wholewheat bread crumbs
⅓ cup grated Parmesan

Salmon and White Wine Parcels

SERVES 4

3–4 garlic cloves, crushed

1 tablespoon honey

1 tablespoon whole-grain Dijon mustard

1 tablespoon balsamic vinegar

2 tablespoons white wine

Zest of 1 lemon

1 small onion, sliced into rings

4 salmon fillets

Small handful of fresh dill, finely chopped

Salt and black pepper, to taste

This recipe takes only minutes to prepare and around 15 minutes to bake. Also, you can prepare the parcels in advance.

- Preheat the halogen oven using the preheat setting, or set the temperature to 400°F.
- Place the garlic, honey, mustard, balsamic vinegar, white wine, and lemon zest in a bowl and mix well.
- Cut 4 squares out of double-thickness aluminum foil, big enough to parcel the salmon fillets.
- Butter the foil and divide the onion rings among the four pieces. Place a salmon fillet over the onions, and then pour the garlic sauce equally over the fillets, ensuring they're well-coated. Add a sprinkle of dill and season to taste.
- Fold the foil over the salmon fillets to create parcels, making sure the edges are well sealed.
- Place on the low rack and cook for 15–20 minutes until the fish flakes easily.
- Unwrap and serve with new potatoes and green vegetables.

Salmon and Shrimp Puff Pie

SERVES 4–6

You can prepare this in advance or freeze until needed.

- Preheat the halogen oven using the preheat setting, or set the temperature to 400°F.
- In a bowl, combine the crème fraîche, milk, and mustard. Season to taste before adding the chopped watercress.
- Place the salmon, shrimp, and spinach in an ovenproof dish and mix well. Pour the crème fraîche mixture into the dish and combine again.
- Roll out the pastry to a $\frac{1}{8}$–$\frac{1}{4}$-inch thickness. Using cookie cutters, cut out small circles of about $1\frac{1}{4}$ inches in diameter.
- Place these pastry circles on the top of the fish mixture, either just around the edges or all over if you prefer. Brush the pastry with a little milk and sprinkle the sesame seeds over the top.
- Place on the low rack and cook for 20–25 minutes until the puff tops have risen and are golden.
- Serve immediately.

1 generous cup crème fraîche or sour cream
1 cup plus 2 tablespoons milk
1 teaspoon whole-grain Dijon mustard
Salt and black pepper, to taste
1½ cups watercress, finely chopped (use arugula or endive if you can't find watercress)
1 lb 2 oz salmon fillets
¾–1 cup shrimp
1½ cups baby leaf spinach, shredded
½ package of ready-to-use puff pastry
Milk for brushing
2 teaspoons of sesame seeds

Vegetarian

Even if you're not vegetarian, I strongly recommend that you eat a vegetable dish at least once or twice a week. The dishes in this chapter are pretty conventional, and although I personally love mung beans, you'll find that the most "adventurous" ingredient included in this chapter's recipes is tofu—so don't be scared!

Some of these recipes can be used as side dishes to accompany a fish or meat meal, while most make wholesome main meals and suppers.

CHAPTER

6

3 large potatoes
2 sweet potatoes
1–2 carrots, cut into
   thin sticks
1–2 leeks, thinly sliced
8–10 small broccoli
   florets (optional)
2 tablespoons butter
¼ cup all-purpose
   flour or cornstarch
1 cup milk
¾ cup–1 cup mature
   Cheddar, grated
1 teaspoon mustard
Salt and black pepper,
   to taste
1–2 large
   tomatoes, sliced
1–2 handfuls of
   spinach leaves

SUITABLE FOR VEGETARIANS

Note: If you don't want
to make a cheese
sauce, you could
simply mix crème
fraîche with some
mature Cheddar.

Eco-warrior Pie

This is a delicious vegetarian version of a British dish known as shepherd's pie, using wonderful, fresh vegetables covered in a cheese sauce and topped with mashed sweet potatoes.

- Use a large steamer to prepare the vegetables; you can steam all of them using one element or ring on your stove top. First, peel and cut the potatoes into equal-sized chunks or slices and steam them for around 10 minutes. Then add the carrot sticks to the steamer on top of the potatoes and steam for 5–10 more minutes. In the last 5–8 minutes of steaming, add the leeks and the broccoli. (This timing assumes that the potatoes will take 20–25 minutes to steam).
- To make the cheese sauce, melt the butter in a saucepan. Add the flour and stir to form a paste. Gradually add the milk and stir well. I find it best to use a whisk at this point since it removes any unwanted lumps. Keep stirring on medium heat until the sauce thickens. Add the grated cheese and mustard and season to taste.
- Mash the potatoes with a little milk or butter and season with black pepper.
- Place the tomato slices on the base of an ovenproof dish or 4–6 individual dishes. Cover with a thin layer of uncooked spinach leaves. Then cover the spinach with the leeks, broccoli, and carrots and coat with the cheese sauce. Finally add the mashed potatoes on top.
- Cook in the halogen oven on the low rack at 400°F for 15 minutes until golden.

Stuffed Mushrooms with Cashews and Parmesan

This is very tasty and can be used as a side dish or main.

- Use a food processor to chop the nuts, onions, and chestnut mushrooms and set aside.
- Combine the bread crumbs with the grated Parmesan and set aside until needed.
- In a sauté or frying pan, add a little olive oil and cook the onions, nuts, and mushrooms for 5 minutes until they begin to soften.
- Preheat the halogen oven using the preheat setting, or set the temperature to 400°F.
- Wash and remove the stalks from the flat mushrooms. Fill them with the onion/cashew mixture. Finish with a generous layer of the breadcrumb and Parmesan mixture.
- Place on the low rack and cook for 15–20 minutes until golden. Serve immediately as a starter or side dish.

SUITABLE FOR VEGETARIANS

¾ cup cashew nuts, finely chopped
1 onion, finely chopped
1 cup chopped chestnut mushrooms
2 cups fresh wholewheat bread crumbs
¾ cup Parmesan cheese, grated
Drizzle of olive oil
4–6 very large, flat mushrooms

Tofu and Garbanzo Burgers

1 x 15-oz can garbanzo
  beans, drained
8 oz of firm tofu
Splash of olive oil
1 onion, finely
  chopped
1–2 garlic cloves,
  crushed
1 chili, finely chopped
1 celery stalk,
  finely chopped
1 teaspoon
  tomato paste
1–2 teaspoons
  garam masala
Splash of soy sauce
Salt and black pepper,
  to taste
1 tablespoon fresh
  wholewheat
  bread crumbs
1 tablespoon
  rolled oats

I love these burgers. Spice them up by doubling the chilies and adding a splash of Tabasco sauce.

- Put the garbanzos in a large bowl and mash until soft. Add the tofu and continue to mash until the two are thoroughly mixed.
- Meanwhile, add a little olive oil to a skillet or frying pan and fry the onion, garlic, chili, and celery until soft. Add this to the chickpea and tofu mixture.
- Add the tomato purée, garam masala, soy sauce, and seasoning. Stir well before adding the bread crumbs and oats.
- Mix thoroughly and form into balls (if the mixture is sticky, do this on a floured surface)—the balls should be firm but moist. Use the palm of your hand to flatten the balls into burger shapes.
- Put them in the refrigerator until ready to use, or freeze them in layers. (Separate each layer with wax paper to prevent them from sticking.)
- When you're ready to cook the burgers, brush them lightly with olive oil.
- Turn the halogen oven to 475°F (or its highest setting). Place the burgers on the high rack and cook/grill for them for 5–8 minutes on each side, until golden.
- Garnish with salad and serve with wholewheat buns.

SUITABLE FOR VEGETARIANS AND VEGANS

Vegetarian Moussaka

A vegetarian version of this tasty dish.

- Put the eggplant slices in a pan of boiling water for 2 minutes. Remove and pat dry. set aside.
- Meanwhile, heat a little olive oil in a skillet or frying pan and fry the onions and garlic. Add the vegetarian ground beef subsitute and cook until brown.
- Add the tomatoes, tomato purée, mint, cinnamon, and seasoning and cook for another 2–3 minutes.
- Select an ovenproof dish—I normally use a Pyrex or lasagne dish for this recipe—and make sure it fits into your halogen oven. Preheat your halogen using the preheat setting, or set the temperature to 400°F.
- Place a layer of "ground beef" in the dish, followed by a layer of eggplant. Continue alternating "ground beef" and eggplant, finishing with a layer of "ground beef".
- Mix the crème fraîche with the grated cheese and pour over the final layer of "ground beef". Garnish with a sprinkle of Parmesan.
- Place on the low rack in the halogen oven and cook for 20–25 minutes until bubbling.

SUITABLE FOR VEGETARIANS

2–3 eggplants, sliced
Splash of olive oil
1 onion, finely chopped
2 garlic cloves, crushed
1 lb vegetarian ground beef substitute
1 x 14.5 oz chopped tomatoes
2 teaspoons tomato paste
1 teaspoon dried mint
2 teaspoons cinnamon
Salt and black pepper, to taste
1¼ cups low-fat crème fraîche or sour cream
½ cup grated mature Cheddar or Parmesan

Mushroom and Goat Cheese Bakes

SERVES 4

2 tablespoons butter
4–6 large portobello
   mushrooms
Dash of olive oil
1 red onion, sliced
2 garlic gloves,
   crushed
2 teaspoons
   balsamic vinegar
2 teaspoons
   brown sugar
1 cup goat cheese,
   crumbled
Black pepper to taste

As a child, I never used to like mushrooms. Thankfully, my tastes have improved and this has now become one of my favorite dishes. You can serve it as a vegetarian alternative to roast meat, or with a salad on a summer day. The combination of red onion, mushroom, and goat cheese is divine!

• Set the halogen oven to 350°F. Put the butter in a small ovenproof bowl and melt for 2 minutes, but don't let it burn.
• Brush the mushrooms with a little melted butter and place on the low rack for 10 minutes.
• In a frying pan, heat a dash of olive oil. Add the onions and garlic and cook until soft. Add the balsamic vinegar and sugar and cook for another 5 minutes to caramelise the onion.
• Remove the mushrooms from the halogen. Add a little of the onion mixture to each mushroom and finish with a crumbling of goat cheese. Season with black pepper.
• Place back in the oven and cook for another 10 minutes, or until the goat cheese is golden.

Note: For added variation, try using crumbled blue cheese instead of goat cheese.

SUITABLE FOR VEGETARIANS

Leek and Cheese Sausages

SERVES 4

Another great meat-free alternative to a traditional roast, or use them for barbecues.

- Put the bread crumbs, oats, cheese, leeks, egg, milk, thyme, and mustard in a bowl and mix well. Season to taste. If the mixture is too wet, add more bread crumbs; if it's too dry, add a little milk. The dough should be firm enough to form thick sausages.
- Put the sausages on a floured sheet of parchment paper and place in the refrigerator to settle for at least 30 minutes.
- When you are ready to cook the sausages, beat the egg in a bowl and, in a second bowl, mix together the farina, oatmeal, flour, and Parmesan. Season to taste.
- Preheat the halogen oven using the preheat setting, or set the temperature to 450°F (or its highest setting).
- Dip each sausage into the egg, and then into the dry mixture. Ensure they are evenly coated. Place on a greased baking sheet or grill tray.
- Place the sausages on the high rack and cook for 5–10 minutes on each side until golden.

SUITABLE FOR VEGETARIANS

2½ cups wholewheat bread crumbs
⅓ cup rolled oats
1½ cups grated mature Cheddar
1 leek, finely chopped
1 egg, beaten
2–2½ tablespoons milk
1 teaspoon dried thyme
1 teaspoon whole grain Dijon mustard
Salt and black pepper, to taste

Coating
1 egg
⅓ cup farina
⅓ cup fine oatmeal
¼ cup all-purpose flour
⅓ cup Parmesan, finely grated
Salt and black pepper, to taste

Basic pizza dough
1 lb 2 oz bread flour
1½ cups warm water
1 package of active
   dried yeast
1 teaspoon
   brown sugar
2 tablespoons olive oil

Homemade Pizza

To save time, make your own pizza dough in advance. Roll it out and place each piece on greased aluminum foil or wax paper. Stack the pizza bases on top of each other, cover in plastic wrap or foil, and refrigerate until ready to use.

• Sift the flour into a bowl.
• Mix the water, yeast, sugar, and oil together. Make sure the sugar is dissolved. Make a well in the middle of the flour and pour this mixture into it.
• Mix thoroughly before transferring the dough onto a floured board. Knead well until the dough springs back when pulled.
• Place the dough in a floured bowl and cover with plastic wrap or a warm, damp cloth until it has doubled in size. This takes about 1 hour.
• Knead again, and divide into individual pizza bases or whatever size you prefer.
• This dough can be stored in the refrigerator or freezer until needed.

SUITABLE FOR VEGETARIANS OR VEGANS
(DEPENDING ON CHOSEN TOPPINGS)

Basic pizza toppings

Pizza toppings can be made using pasta sauce or even simple tomato paste mixed with olive oil and herbs. There are no hard-and-fast rules for pizza toppings, so experiment with whatever you like and have fun. Below are some suggestions to help you but, really, anything goes!

Tomato and cheese
Pepperoni, mushroom, red onion, and cheese
Ham and mushroom
Ham, pineapple, and cheese
Sausage, jalapeño, tomato, and cheese
Red onion, black olive, tomato, cheese, and red pepper
Roasted vegetables

Bake your pizza
- Once your dough has proved, roll it out to the desired thickness and size. Cover it with your desired toppings, starting with the tomato base.
- I normally cook my pizza directly on the lower rack as I like the bottom to be crisp, but you can place it on a tray or on foil directly on the rack.
- Turn the halogen oven to 400°F and cook for 10–15 minutes until golden.
- Due to the force of the fan, if you have loose toppings you may want to place the high rack face down on top of the pizza—first spray the rack with a little oil to prevent it from sticking. You only need to do this for the first half of the cooking time.

SERVES 4–6

1 package of cherry
   tomatoes, halved
2–3 garlic cloves,
   crushed
1 red or Spanish
   onion, sliced
1 teaspoon salt
1 teaspoon sugar
Handful of crushed
   fresh basil leaves
Drizzle of olive oil
1 ball of mozzarella or
   ¾ cup goat cheese,
   crumbled (omit if
   vegan and substitute
   with vegan cheese
   if desired)

Basic dough
1 lb 2 oz bread flour
1½ cups warm water
1 packageof active
   dried yeast
1 teaspoon
   brown sugar
2 tablespoons olive oil

Upside-down Pizza Bake

This is a really nice dish and makes a change from the normal pizza. It uses the same principle as an upside down cake. This recipe uses cherry tomatoes, but feel free to use a variety of your choice.

- Place the tomatoes, garlic, onions, salt, sugar, basil, and olive oil on a deep-sided baking sheet. Ideally choose a round one, so that you can turn this out onto a serving plate when complete, but make sure it fits in your halogen oven!
- Cook at 250–275°F for 40–50 minutes.
- Meanwhile, prepare the dough. Sift the flour into a bowl. Mix the water, yeast, sugar, and oil together. Make sure the sugar is dissolved. Make a well in the middle of the flour and pour this mixture into it.
- Mix thoroughly before transferring the dough onto a floured board. Knead well until the dough springs back when pulled.
- Place the dough in a floured bowl and cover with plastic wrap or a warm, damp cloth until it has doubled in size. This takes about 1 hour.
- Knead again. Roll out to the same size as your baking sheet (you will later place the dough inside the tray to form a top). You may have more dough then needed—it depends on how thick you want the crust of the bake. If you have some left over, roll it out to make a pizza base—cover this in greased foil or parchment paper and freeze for another day.
- Remove the baked tomatoes from the halogen oven and turn up the temperature to 400°F. Top the tomatoes with the dough; cheese-lovers may like to

add some crumbled mozzarella or even goat cheese onto the tomatoes before adding the dough.

- Put this back into the halogen oven and bake for 15–20 minutes, until the top is golden.
- To serve, place a plate, slightly larger than the top of the baking sheet, over the dough, face down. Then flip the tray and remove it to display the tomato base on top of the pizza dough.
- Serve with green salad.

SUITABLE FOR VEGETARIANS OR VEGANS

Sun-dried Tomato and Goat Cheese Frittata

SERVES 4–6

- Preheat the halogen oven using the preheat setting, or set the temperature to 400°F.
- Beat the eggs well in a large bowl. Add the remaining ingredients and combine. Pour into a well-greased ovenproof dish.
- Place on the low rack and cook for 20–25 minutes until firm.
- Serve hot or cold with salad.

SUITABLE FOR VEGETARIANS

5 eggs
4–5 scallions (spring onions), finely chopped
1 cup goat cheese, crumbled
4–6 sun-dried tomatoes, chopped
1 teaspoon mixed dried herbs
Salt and black pepper, to taste

Slow-baked Tomato, Pepper, and Basil Soup

SERVES 4

8 tomatoes, quartered
1 red bell pepper,
   quartered
2–4 garlic cloves,
   crushed
Sprinkle of sea salt
Sprinkle of sugar
Small handful of
   fresh basil leaves
   (or thyme)
Drizzle of olive oil
2 cups vegetable stock
   or water
1 teaspoon sun-dried
   tomato paste
2–3 teaspoons of
   freshly chopped basil
Salt and black pepper,
   to taste

This is a really tasty soup. For a more wholesome version, add a quarter to a third of a cup dried red lentils. Just boil them in water until soft, add with the water, and blitz until smooth.

• Put the chopped tomatoes, pepper, and garlic directly in your halogen bowl (or use a baking sheet if you prefer). Sprinkle with sea salt, sugar, and basil leaves and drizzle with olive oil. Turn the halogen oven to 325°F and cook for 30 minutes.
• Remove the vegetables from the halogen and mix in the stock. Add more water or stock if necessary (or add the cooked lentils along with the stock or water). Add the tomato paste and chopped basil. Mix until smooth with an electric hand blender. Season to taste.
• Serve with fresh bread for a tasty lunch or light evening meal.

SUITABLE FOR VEGETARIANS

Roasted Pumpkin Soup

SERVES 4–6

This makes a delicious treat for Halloween. For an all-year treat, use other kinds of squash.

- Preheat the halogen oven using the preheat setting, or set the temperature to 400°F.
- Put the pumpkin, sweet potato, and carrot wedges on a baking sheet and brush lightly with oil. Add the onions, garlic, and spices and mix well.
- Place on the low rack and bake for 20 minutes.
- Remove the skin from the pumpkin wedges and roughly chop the roasted vegetables. Place them with the onion and seasoning mix in a casserole dish. Add all the remaining ingredients and mix well.
- Place the casserole dish on the low rack. Cover with a lid or with aluminum foil secured tightly. Cook at 400°F for 30–40 minutes.
- Cool slightly and then use an electric hand blender to purée. Season as required.
- For impressive presentation, use hollowed-out pumpkins as serving dishes.

SUITABLE FOR VEGETARIANS AND VEGANS

1 small pumpkin, cut
  into wedges
1 medium
  sweet potato, cut
  into wedges
1–2 carrots,
  thickly chopped
  into wedges
Olive oil to brush
1 onion
1–2 garlic
  cloves, crushed
1 teaspoon grated
  fresh ginger
1 teaspoon
  grated nutmeg
1 teaspoon coriander
2 celery stalks
4 tomatoes, peeled
  and chopped
2 teaspoons of tomato
  paste (optional)
1¼–2 cups water
  or stock
1 tablespoon
  lemon juice
Salt and black pepper,
  to taste

1–2 butternut
squash, halved
Drizzle of olive oil
Sprinkle of paprika
Salt and black pepper,
to taste
1 red or Spanish
onion, finely
chopped
2–3 garlic cloves,
crushed
½ cup cashews,
finely chopped
1¼ cups finely
chopped mushrooms
1 cup goat cheese,
crumbled

Butternut Squash Stuffed with Mushroom, Cashews, and Goat Cheese

- Preheat the halogen oven using the preheat setting, or set the temperature to 375°F.
- While the oven is heating, halve the butternut squash and remove the seeds. Using a sharp knife, scour the flesh in a crisscross pattern, then put the squash on a greased baking sheet and brush with olive oil and a sprinkle of paprika. Season to taste.
- Place on the low rack and cook for 30 minutes.
- Meanwhile, put the onion, garlic, cashews, and mushrooms in a food processor and blitz until roughly chopped. Alternatively, roughly chop by hand.
- Place this chopped mushroom mixture in a skillet or frying pan and fry in a little olive oil for 3–4 minutes. set aside until needed.
- When the butternut squash is soft, remove it from the oven. Scoop out a little of the flesh from each half of the squash to form a small well in the center. Add this to the mushroom mixture.
- Spoon the mushroom mixture onto the butternut squash, and finish with a scattering of crumbled goat cheese. Place the squash back in the halogen oven on the low rack for 10–15 minutes until golden.
- Serve with a fresh green salad.

SUITABLE FOR VEGETARIANS

Vegetable Mornay Bake

SERVES 4-6

- Chop the carrots into sticks, slice the leeks and cut the broccoli and cauliflower into florets. Put in a steamer and cook until the cauliflower is tender but not soft.
- Meanwhile, make the sauce. Melt the butter gently in a saucepan on your stove top on medium heat. Add the flour or cornstarch and stir well with a wooden spoon. Add the milk a little at a time, stirring continuously to avoid lumps.
- Switch to a whisk. Continue to stir over medium heat until the sauce begins to thicken. Add more milk as necessary to get the desired thickness—the sauce should have the consistency of custard.
- Add $\frac{3}{4}$ cup of the cheese and the mustard and stir well. Season with black pepper.
- Preheat the halogen oven using the preheat setting, or set the temperature to 400°F.
- When the vegetables are ready, transfer them to an ovenproof dish. Pour the sauce over the vegetables, making sure they're all covered.
- Mix the bread crumbs, oats, and Parmesan together thoroughly. Scatter over the cheese sauce.
- Place the mornay on the low rack. Cook for 15–20 minutes until the top is golden and crispy.

SUITABLE FOR VEGETARIANS

2 carrots
2 leeks
1 small head
   of broccoli
1 small cauliflower
2 tablespoons butter
1 tablespoon all-
   purpose flour or
   cornstarch
2–3 cups milk
1 cup grated mature
   Cheddar ($\frac{3}{4}$ for
   the sauce, $\frac{1}{4}$ for
   the topping)
$\frac{1}{2}$ teaspoon
   dry mustard
Black pepper to taste
2–3 tablespoons
   fresh wholewheat
   bread crumbs
2 tablespoons
   rolled oats
$\frac{1}{4}$ cup grated
   Parmesan cheese

Leek, Mushroom, and Blue Cheese Parcels

SERVES 4

Olive oil, for frying
1 leek, finely chopped
1 cup quartered
  chestnut mushrooms
Black pepper to taste
8–12 large
  cabbage leaves
½–¾ cup crumbled
  blue cheese
¼–⅓ cup pine nuts
Salt and black pepper,
  to taste

These flavors were made for each other. This is a great, filling dish, suitable as a main meal for vegetarians or as a side dish.

- Heat the oil in a skillet or frying pan and fry the leeks for 2 minutes. Add the mushrooms and fry for 1 minute. Season with black pepper and set aside.
- Meanwhile, put the cabbage leaves in a pan of boiling water for 2–3 minutes to soften. Remove and pat dry with paper towels.
- Place some of the leek and mushroom filling in the center of each leaf, then sprinkle with a little of the cheese and pine nuts and roll into a parcel. If you need to, use a wooden toothpick to help secure the leaves in place.
- Place the cabbage parcel on a greased square of aluminum foil. Bring the sides of the foil up to form a well. Add 2 teaspoons of water, then secure the foil to form a parcel. Repeat this with all the cabbage parcels.
- Once all the cabbage leaves are parcelled, you can put them in and around other food in the halogen, or put them on the low rack.
- Cook at 450°F for 15 minutes. Unwrap and serve.

SUITABLE FOR VEGETARIANS

Roasted Tomato and Garlic Peppers

I love this dish. You can serve it with a selection of salads or even just some gorgeous homemade bread. If you want to add Parmesan, mozzarella, or goat cheese, do so in the last 10 minutes of cooking.

- Preheat the halogen oven using the preheat setting, or set the temperature to 350°F.
- Halve the peppers and remove the seeds. Brush with a little olive oil and place in an ovenproof dish, first making sure it fits well in your halogen.
- Put the tomato halves in the halved peppers. Sprinkle with the garlic and thyme leaves.
- In a bowl or cup, mix the olive oil with the balsamic vinegar. Pour a little of this mixture onto each pepper half. Finish with a sprinkle of sea salt, sugar, and black pepper.
- Bake the peppers on the low rack for 40 minutes, until they are soft. If you want to crumble some cheese over the top, do it now and cook for 10 more minutes.
- Serve in the dish, mopping up any juice with bread or salad.

SUITABLE FOR VEGETARIANS AND VEGANS

SERVES 4–6

4 red bell peppers
Olive oil, to brush
12 cherry tomatoes, halved
4–6 garlic cloves, roughly chopped
4–6 sprigs of fresh thyme
1–2 tablespoons olive oil
2 teaspoons balsamic vinegar
Sprinkle of sea salt
Sprinkle of sugar
Sprinkle of black pepper

Leek and Quorn Pie

This is a bit like a traditional chicken pie but, using Quorn, it is suitable for vegetarians.

SERVES 4–6

1 large potato, cubed
2–3 carrots, sliced
Splash of olive oil
1 onion, finely
  chopped
1–2 garlic cloves
  (optional)
2 leeks, finely chopped
6–7 oz Quorn (or
  other vegetable
  protein/ground
  beef subsitute)
8 oz ricotta cheese
  mixed with
  1 oz of sour cream
3 tablespoons
  Greek yogurt
¾ cup grated mature
  Cheddar (optional)
Salt and black pepper,
  to taste
Small handful of fresh
  tarragon, chopped,
  or 1 teaspoon dried
½ package of
  puff pastry
1 tablespoon milk
Handful of sesame
  seeds for sprinkling

- Steam the potato cubes and carrots for 10 minutes.
- Meanwhile, heat the oil in a large skillet or frying pan and fry the onions, garlic, and leeks for 5 minutes to soften.
- Add the Quorn or vegetable protein and cook for 5 minutes, then turn off the heat. Add the ricotta/sour cream mixture and the yogurt (and the cheese if you are using it).
- When the potato and carrot are cooked, add them to the leek mixture. Season and add the herbs.
- Put the mixture in an ovenproof pie plate. Roll out the pastry to a size larger than required. Wet the edges of the dish with milk or water, and cut thin strips of pastry to place around the edge—dampen again with milk. This will give the top pastry something to hold on to. Cut the top pastry to size and place over the pie. Crimp and seal the edges.
- Brush with milk and sprinkle with sesame seeds. Cut 2 holes in the middle of the pastry to allow the pie to breathe.
- Place on the low rack and set the temperature to 400°F. Bake for 20–30 minutes until the pie crust is golden.
- Serve with roast new potatoes and green vegetables.

SUITABLE FOR VEGETARIANS

Stuffed Peppers with Goat Cheese

A simple dish—perfect for summer evenings with a selection of salad dishes.

- Preheat the halogen oven using the preheat setting, or set the temperature to 350°F.
- Cut the peppers in half and remove the seeds. Brush with olive oil, place in an ovenproof dish, and bake on the low rack in the halogen oven for 10 minutes.
- Meanwhile, mix the cooked rice or couscous with the scallions, cherry tomatoes, walnuts, and parsley. Season to taste.
- Remove the peppers from the oven and turn up the temperature to 400°F.
- Stuff the peppers with the rice mixture and finish with a layer of goat cheese.
- Bake on the low rack for 10–15 minutes until the cheese is starting to brown and bubble.

SUITABLE FOR VEGETARIANS

SERVES 4–6

4 peppers
Olive oil, for brushing
1½ cups cooked rice
 or couscous
Bunch of scallions
 (spring onions),
 chopped
12 cherry
 tomatoes, chopped
½ cup chopped
 walnuts
Small handful chopped
 fresh parsley
Salt and black pepper,
 to taste
1¼ cups goat cheese

Spinach and Ricotta Lasagne

SERVES 4–6

1 onion, finely
chopped
1 cup of ricotta
1 cup grated
mature Cheddar
6 oz or about 4½ cups
fresh spinach leaves
(baby spinach is best)
¼ teaspoon
grated nutmeg
Black pepper to taste
Lasagne sheets
1 x 14–15 oz jar
of pasta sauce
Grated Parmesan
or other cheese,
for topping

We eat this dish at least twice a month. It has some great flavors, so even if you aren't vegetarian, give it a try. Unlike most lasagne dishes, it takes minutes to prepare.

- Put the onions, ricotta, and Cheddar in a bowl and mix well. Add the spinach leaves. (If you put the spinach in a colander and run it under hot water for a few seconds, the leaves will soften. This makes the mixing easier.)
- Add the grated nutmeg and season with black pepper.
- Preheat the halogen oven using the preheat setting, or set the temperature to 400°F.
- Put a thin layer of the ricotta mixture in the bottom of a lasagne dish, followed by a layer of lasagne sheets. Top with a thin layer of pasta sauce. Continue with a layer of ricotta, then lasagne, and finally the remaining pasta sauce. Add approximately 2 tablespoons of water to the empty pasta sauce jar, swirl it around, then pour the water over the top of the lasagne.
- Grate some Parmesan (or other cheese of your choice) onto the lasagne and season.
- Place in the halogen oven on the low rack and cook for 40–50 minutes. If the top starts to get too dark, cover it with aluminum foil, making sure the foil is secure.
- Serve with potato wedges and salad—delicious!

SUITABLE FOR VEGETARIANS

Tomato and Mozzarella Puffs

Puff pastry is the busy cook's best friend. You can create your own toppings, but this is simple favorite will get you started.

- Roll out the pastry to a ⅛–¼–inch thickness and cut it into 4–6 squares. Carefully score around the edge of each square, half an inch from the edge of the pastry. Don't cut the pastry, just make a slight indent.
- Preheat the halogen oven using the preheat setting, or set the temperature to 400°F.
- In the middle of each pastry square add 1 teaspoon of sun-dried tomato paste and spread evenly within the scored line. Put pieces of mozzarella and a few leaves of basil inside the scored line. Add a few cherry tomatoes, halved or whole, depending on your preference. Season to taste.
- Place on a lined or well-greased baking sheet and place on the high rack. Bake for about 15 minutes until the pastry is golden. If the tarts start to brown before the base is cooked, transfer them to the low rack for a few more minutes.
- Before serving, add a garnish of basil leaves.

SUITABLE FOR VEGETARIANS

½ package of store-bought puff pastry
4 teaspoons sun-dried tomato paste
4–5 oz mozzarella, sliced
Handful of fresh basil leaves
8–10 cherry tomatoes
Salt and black pepper, to taste

Slow-baked Tomatoes

6–8 large, ripe
  tomatoes, halved
  (or 12–14
  cherry tomatoes)
4 garlic cloves,
  crushed (more
  if preferred)
1 teaspoon salt
1 teaspoon sugar
Sprinkle of
  balsamic vinegar
Drizzle of olive oil
Handful of fresh herbs
  (basil or oregano)

You can use this as a quick and easy pasta sauce, a pizza topping, an accompaniment to a meat, fish, or vegetable dish, or in a salad. The sweetness of the tomatoes alongside the hit of basil and garlic is heavenly. I bake this in large batches, especially when I have ripe tomatoes that need using up, or if I see cherry tomatoes on offer. You can then store it in jars (covered in olive oil) or in an airtight container in the refrigerator for up to a week.

- Preheat the halogen oven using the preheat setting, or set the temperature to 125°C.
- Place the tomatoes in a baking sheet. Sprinkle with the garlic, salt, sugar, and balsamic vinegar. Finish with a drizzle of olive oil.
- Place in the oven on the low rack for 1 hour.
- When cooked, add a handful of fresh herbs. I prefer oregano or fresh basil.
- Use or store as required.

SUITABLE FOR VEGETARIANS AND VEGANS

Cheese and Potato Puffs

Perfect for picnics or packed lunches.

- Cook and mash the potatoes.
- Place the potatoes, diced onion, grated carrot, and cheese in a bowl and mix thoroughly. Add two-thirds of the beaten eggs and the herbs and season well.
- Roll out the pastry on a floured surface until even. Cut into 4-inch squares.
- Preheat the halogen oven using the preheat setting, or set the temperature to 400°F.
- Place some of the cheese and potato mixture in the center of each square—do not overfill. Use a little of the remaining beaten egg to brush the edges of the pastry before bringing the edges together to form a triangle. Crimp until sealed.
- Put the pasties on a lined baking sheet. Brush with the remaining beaten egg and bake on the low rack for 20–25 minutes until the pastry is golden and flaky.

SUITABLE FOR VEGETARIANS

½–1 package of store-
  bought puff pastry
3–4 potatoes, cooked
  and mashed (or use
  leftover mash)
1 onion, diced
1 carrot, grated
1½ cups grated
  mature Cheddar
3 eggs, beaten
1 teaspoon mixed
  herbs (optional)
Salt and black pepper,
  to taste

Tofu and Blue Cheese Quiche

SERVES 4–6

1 cup all-purpose flour
2 tablespoons
  cold butter
5–6 tablespoons cold
  water
1 box tofu, mashed
1¼ cups grated mature
  Cheddar
1 onion, finely
  chopped
Splash of milk '
  (if needed)
Salt and black pepper,
  to taste
⅓–½ cup blue cheese

This quiche is one of my favorites, and it's a big hit with meat-eaters as well as vegetarians—most don't realize they're eating tofu! It can be adapted for vegans by using vegan cheeses.

- First, make the pastry. Put the flour in a large bowl and add small pieces of the chilled butter. Using your fingertips, rub the butter into the flour until the whole mix resembles bread crumbs. Add the water (a little at a time) and mix until a dough is formed. Wrap the dough in plastic wrap and put in the refrigerator to cool until needed.
- Preheat the halogen oven using the preheat setting, or set the temperature to 400°F.
- Roll out the pastry on a floured surface to the size and thickness needed to line a 9-inch greased quiche or tart pan. Place a sheet of parchment paper over the pastry and cover with baking weights or dried beans.
- Bake for 10 minutes. Remove the baking weights/beans and parchment and cook for a further 5 minutes. Remove the pastry shell from the halogen and turn the oven down to 350°F.
- Meanwhile, mash the tofu thoroughly. Add the grated cheese and onions. If the mixture is too dry, add a splash of milk and mix well. Season well before pouring into the pastry shell. Cover with a sprinkling of crumbled blue cheese, then place the pan on the high rack.
- Bake in the oven for 20 minutes, until golden.

SUITABLE FOR VEGETARIANS

Spinach and Feta Pie

SERVES 4–6

Serve this with a selection of fresh salads and new potatoes—it's perfect for a summer evening.

- Preheat the halogen oven using the preheat setting, or set the temperature to 400°F.
- Melt the butter in a saucepan on your stove top or put it in a bowl in your halogen oven to melt.
- Layer 3 sheets of pastry in the base of a pie plate. Brush butter between the sheets and allow them to hang over the edge of the dish to give you enough pastry to form the sides of the pie.
- Put a thin layer of spinach leaves on the pastry, followed by a layer of crumbled feta. Season with black pepper and nutmeg. Repeat this, finishing with a feta layer.
- Cover with more phyllo sheets, again brushing with butter in between. Bring the edges together to form a crust and remove any excess pastry.
- Brush with butter and sprinkle with sesame seeds.
- Place on the low rack and bake for 30–40 minutes until golden.

SUITABLE FOR VEGETARIANS

3 tablespoons butter
6 sheets of
   phyllo pastry
1 lb baby leaf spinach,
   roughly torn
1¼ cups feta
   cheese, crumbled
Black pepper,
   to season
¼ teaspoon
   grated nutmeg
Sesame seeds,
   to sprinkle

SERVES 4–6

2 tablespoons butter

4–6 large portobello mushrooms

2 tablespoons milk

1 cup grated mature Cheddar

1 teaspoon dry mustard

Salt and black pepper, to taste

Baked Mushroom Rarebit

Cheese and mushrooms are a match made in heaven. Serve as a main dish with vegetables, or as a snack with toast triangles.

- Set the halogen oven to 350°F. Put the butter in a small ovenproof bowl and melt it in the halogen for 2–3 minutes, but don't let it burn.
- Brush the mushrooms with a little melted butter and place them on the low rack for 8–10 minutes.
- In a saucepan on your stove top, add the milk, remaining butter, cheese, and mustard. Stir until the ingredients are dissolved and thick. Be careful not to have the temperature too high or it will stick and burn.
- Pour the cheesy mixture over the mushrooms. Season to taste. Place on the high rack and cook on high heat (400–475°F) for 5 minutes, until golden and bubbling.

SUITABLE FOR VEGETARIANS

Vegetable Cheesy Cobbler

SERVES 4

- Chop the vegetables and place them in a steamer. Steam until soft.
- Meanwhile, make the sauce. Melt the butter gently in a saucepan on your stove top on medium heat. Add the flour or cornstarch and stir well with a wooden spoon. Add the milk a little at a time, stirring continuously to avoid lumps.
- Switch now to a whisk. Continue to stir over medium heat until the sauce begins to thicken.
- Add the Cheddar and mustard and stir well. Season with black pepper.
- Preheat the oven using the preheat setting or set the temperature to 350°F.
- Place the self-rising flour and Parmesan in a bowl and season to taste. Create a well in the center and add the oil and yogurt. Stir well to form a dough.
- Roll out the dough on a floured surface to a 1¼–2-inch thickness. Use cookie cutters to create biscuit-size rounds.
- Place the vegetables in the base of an ovenproof dish. Pour over the cheese sauce and put the "biscuits" around the edge of the dish. Brush the dough with a little milk and sprinkle with sesame seeds. Put the dish in the oven and bake on the low rack for 25–30 minutes.

SUITABLE FOR VEGETARIANS

2 leeks, finely sliced
2 carrots, cut into sticks
½ head of broccoli
½ head of cauliflower
2 tablespoons butter
25g all-purpose flour (or cornstarch)
2–3 cups milk
1 cup grated mature Cheddar
½ teaspoon dry mustard
Salt and black pepper, to taste
1 cup self-rising flour
Scant ½ cup finely grated Parmesan cheese
2 tablespoons olive oil
3 tablespoons natural yogurt
Sprinkle of sesame seeds

Roasted Mediterranean-style Vegetables

2–3 red onions, quartered
1 whole garlic bulb, broken into cloves
2 eggplant, cut into thick chunks
1 fennel bulb, quartered, then halved again
2 red bell peppers, quartered
Drizzle of olive oil
3 tablespoons balsamic vinegar
Small handful fresh basil leaves
Sprigs of fresh thyme
Salt and black pepper, to taste
4–6 vine tomatoes
Sprinkle of sugar

The halogen lends itself so well to roasting. This is a delicious dish and can be used a bit like ratatouille.

- Preheat the halogen oven using the preheat setting, or set the temperature to 400°F.
- Place all the prepared vegetables, except the tomatoes, into a roasting/baking or ovenproof pan.
- Drizzle with olive oil and balsamic vinegar and scatter with the basil leaves and thyme sprigs. Season to taste.
- Place on the low rack and cook for 20 minutes.
- Sprinkle the tomatoes with a very small amount of sugar, then remove the pan and add the tomatoes. Stir the vegetables, ensuring they are coated in oil and balsamic.
- Turn the temperature down to 350°F. Place the vegetables back into the halogen on the low rack for another 20 minutes until cooked.

SUITABLE FOR VEGETARIANS AND VEGANS

Ratatouille and Feta Gratin

SERVES 4

I love the crispy topping of this dish.

- Preheat the halogen oven using the preheat setting, or turn the temperature to 400°F.
- Place all the prepared vegetables in an ovenproof dish. Add the olive oil, sugar, balsamic vinegar, wine, herbs, and seasoning. Mix to ensure all the vegetables are covered in a little oil.
- Bake on the low rack for 20–30 minutes, until the vegetables are soft.
- Meanwhile, mix together the bread crumbs, oats, and Parmesan. Season to taste.
- Remove the vegetables from the oven and stir in the feta cheese. Finish with the bread-crumb mix.
- Return to the low rack and cook for another 15 minutes, until golden.

SUITABLE FOR VEGETARIANS

1 eggplant, diced
1 red onion, sliced
2 garlic cloves, crushed
1 red bell pepper, roughly diced
1 courgette, diced
8 ripe tomatoes, quartered (or use canned if you prefer)
Olive oil
Sprinkle of sugar
2–3 teaspoons balsamic vinegar
½ cup red wine
Sprigs of thyme
Small handful of bay leaves
Salt and black pepper, to taste
1½ cups fresh wholewheat bread crumbs
½ cup rolled oats
½ cup grated Parmesan cheese
1¼ cups feta cheese, crumbled

SERVES 4–6

4–6 beefsteak
  tomatoes
Drizzle of olive oil
1 red onion, finely
  chopped
2–3 garlic cloves,
  crushed
½ red pepper
¼ cup pine nuts
Small handful of basil
  leaves, chopped
¼–⅓ cup dry couscous
Salt and black pepper,
  to taste
½ cup mozzarella,
  crumbled

Stuffed Tomatoes

Perfect for a summer evening with new potatoes and various salad dishes.

- Preheat the halogen oven using the preheat setting, or turn the temperature to 350°F.
- Carefully cut off the tops of the tomatoes and scoop out the flesh. Chop the removed tops finely and place them, along with the flesh, in a bowl. Put the tomato shells on a baking sheet and set aside.
- In a skillet or frying pan, fry the onion and the garlic in a little olive oil for a couple of minutes. Then add the red pepper and cook until soft.
- Remove from the heat and add to the bowl of tomato flesh. Add the pine nuts and basil leaves.
- Re-hydrate the couscous following the instructions on the package, then add it to the bowl. Season to taste and stir well to combine all the ingredients.
- Place this mixture in your tomato shells, finishing with some crumbled mozzarella. Sprinkle with black pepper before placing on the low rack and cooking for 25–30 minutes.

SUITABLE FOR VEGETARIANS

Spicy Butternut Squash

If you haven't tried butternut squash before, do so. It is really delicious—and this is a very simple dish to prepare.

- Preheat the halogen oven using the preheat setting, or set the temperature to 375°F.
- Halve the butternut squash and remove the seeds. Using a sharp knife, scour the flesh in a crisscross pattern. Place the squash on a greased baking sheet. Brush with olive oil and a sprinkle of paprika.
- Place on the low rack and cook for 30 minutes.
- Meanwhile, in a skillet or frying pan, fry the onions, garlic, and chili in a little oil until they start to soften. Add the curry powder and red pepper and cook for another couple of minutes before adding all remaining ingredients, apart from the cheese.
- Cook for another 5 minutes, making sure the ingredients are thoroughly mixed. Set aside.
- When the butternut squash is soft, remove it from the oven. Scoop out a little of the flesh to form a small well in the center of each half. Add this to the bean mixture, then spoon the bean mixture into the squash.
- If you like cheesy chili flavors, scatter grated cheese over the top of each squash before putting them back in the halogen oven. Cook on the low rack for 10–15 minutes until golden.
- Serve with a green salad.

SUITABLE FOR VEGETARIANS AND VEGANS

1–2 butternut squash
Brush of olive oil
Sprinkle of paprika
1 red or Spanish
  onion, finely
  chopped
2–3 garlic
  cloves, crushed
1 chili, finely chopped
1–2 teaspoons mild
  curry powder
1 red pepper,
  finely chopped
1 x 14.5 oz chopped
  tomatoes
1 x 14-15-oz can mixed
  beans, drained
Small handful of
  coriander leaves,
  finely chopped
Salt and black
  pepper, to taste
Grated cheese
  (optional—omit for
  a vegan version)

Spinach and Ricotta Cannelloni

SERVES 4–6

6 oz (about 5 cups) fresh baby leaf spinach (or 10 oz frozen spinach)

1 cup of ricotta

¼ teaspoon grated nutmeg

6–8 cannelloni tubes or lasagne sheets

1 small red or Spanish onion

2 garlic cloves, crushed

Drizzle of olive oil

1 x 14.5 oz chopped tomatoes

¼ cup red wine

Handful of freshly chopped basil leaves

Salt and black pepper, to taste

Grated Parmesan, to sprinkle

This is such a simple dish to make, but it looks impressive and tastes even better!

- Put the spinach in a colander and run it under hot water for a couple of minutes to soften the leaves. If using frozen spinach, allow it to defrost before moving on to the next step.
- In a bowl, mix the ricotta, spinach, and nutmeg. Using a teaspoon, fill the cannelloni tubes with the ricotta mixture. Place the stuffed tubes in an ovenproof dish in a single layer. (If you want to speed up the cooking time, use fresh cannelloni tubes. If using dried lasagne sheets, first cook them in boiling water for 5–8 minutes, then drain. Add the ricotta mixture to one end of the sheets. Roll them up firmly to form tubes and place them seal-side down on the bottom of the ovenproof dish.)
- Preheat the halogen oven using the preheat setting, or set the temperature to 375°F.
- Fry the onions and garlic in a little olive oil to soften. Add the tomatoes, wine, basil leaves, and seasoning and cook for a couple of minutes before pouring over the cannelloni.
- Sprinkle with Parmesan before placing on the low rack. Cook for 35–40 minutes, or until the cannelloni is cooked. (This takes 20–25 minutes if using fresh pasta or lasagne sheets as described above.)
- Serve with some garlic bread and green salad.

SUITABLE FOR VEGETARIANS

Roasted Vegetable and Garbanzo Salad

You can prepare the roasted vegetables in advance and leave them in the refrigerator until needed.

- Preheat the halogen oven using the preheat setting, or set the temperature to 400°F.
- Prepare the onion, peppers, and tomatoes (leaving aside the cherry tomatoes for now) and put on a baking sheet. Drizzle with olive oil and sprinkle with sugar and a little salt. Add the thyme and rosemary leaves.
- Place on the low rack and cook for 20 minutes, until the vegetables are soft.
- Remove from the heat and place in a bowl. (You can serve this dish hot or cold—it's your choice, but I prefer it hot.) Add the drained garbanzo beans, halved cherry tomatoes, and chopped mint leaves.
- Mix the olive oil, white-wine vinegar, crushed garlic, and lemon juice in a bowl. Season to taste. Pour this over the vegetable mixture and mix well.

SUITABLE FOR VEGETARIANS AND VEGANS

12 small red or Spanish onions, cut into wedges
2 bell peppers, thickly sliced
4 tomatoes, quartered
Drizzle of olive oil
1 teaspoon sugar
Sprinkle of salt
Small handful of fresh rosemary and thyme sprigs
1 x 15 oz can garbanzo beans, drained
4–6 cherry tomatoes, halved
Small handful of fresh mint leaves, chopped
2 tablespoons olive oil
2 tablespoons white-wine vinegar
2 garlic cloves, crushed
Juice of ½ a lemon
Salt and black pepper, to taste

Slow-cooked Basil and Tomato Pasta Bake with Feta

SERVES 4

8–10 ripe
tomatoes, quartered
3–4 garlic
cloves, crushed
2 red or Spanish
onions, cut
into wedges
1–2 red bell peppers,
thickly sliced
Handful of fresh
basil leaves
Drizzle of olive oil
2 teaspoons
balsamic vinegar
1 teaspoon sugar
1 teaspoon salt
10 oz (about 3 cups)
penne pasta
2 cups cubed
feta cheese
Olives, chopped
(optional)

This dish was invented by accident. While I was preparing slow-baked tomatoes for a soup, my family declared they'd rather have pasta for dinner! Fortunately it turned out well and is now a family favorite. I hope you enjoy it. If there is any leftover slow-cooked tomatoes, store them in the refrigerator and use as a pizza topping.

• Preheat the halogen oven using the preheat setting, or set the temperature to 325°F.
• In an ovenproof dish, combine the tomatoes, garlic, onion, red peppers, and half the basil leaves. Drizzle with oil and balsamic vinegar and sprinkle with sugar and a little salt.
• Place on the low rack and cook for 30 minutes.
• Timing is everything here, so when you're ready to serve, cook the pasta as per the instructions on the package. It won't hurt to cook the tomato mixture in advance and leave it until you're ready to continue. Just reheat the tomatoes 5 minutes before the pasta is ready.
• Drain the cooked pasta and put it with the tomato mixture in an ovenproof dish. Stir in the feta cubes and olives. Place back in the halogen oven on the low rack and cook for 10 minutes at 375°F.
• Serve with a green salad.

SUITABLE FOR VEGETARIANS

Roasted Butternut, Spinach, and Goat Cheese Layer

This may take a little time to prepare but, other than chopping, the halogen does all the hard work for you. It tastes amazing and will impress even the most dedicated meat-eaters!

- Preheat the halogen oven using the preheat setting, or set the temperature to 400°F.
- Prepare your vegetables. In a pestle and mortar, roughly grind the coriander and cumin seeds.
- Place the squash slices on a baking sheet and drizzle with olive oil. Sprinkle with the coriander seeds, cumin, and chili.
- Put the vegetables on a baking sheet (or directly on the low rack) and roast for 15 minutes. Add the onion and garlic and put back in the oven for another 15 minutes.
- Meanwhile, prepare the rest of the layers. Rinse the spinach leaves under hot water to soften the leaves. Put the leaves in a bowl and mix in the ricotta. Season to taste and set aside.
- Remove the squash from the oven. Drain off any excess oil and combine the squash, onion and garlic together. Place half of this in the bottom of an ovenproof dish.
- Add a layer of the spinach and ricotta mix. Follow this with a layer of sliced tomatoes, the rest of the squash, the ricotta mixture, and pine nuts and finish with the crumbled goat cheese.
- Place on the low rack and bake for 20 minutes.
- Serve with a selection of delicious salads.

SUITABLE FOR VEGETARIANS

---

1 butternut squash, peeled, deseeded, and sliced
Drizzle of olive oil
2 teaspoons coriander seeds
1 teaspoon cumin
1–2 chilies, finely chopped (depending on desired strength)
2 red or Spanish onions, sliced
3–4 garlic cloves, chopped
2–3 cups baby leaf spinach
1 cup of ricotta
Salt and black pepper, to taste
1–2 ripe tomatoes, sliced
¼ cup pine nuts
1 cup goat cheese, crumbled

SERVES 4–6

1 sweet potato, diced
1 potato, diced
2 carrots, diced
Drizzle of olive oil
1 onion, finely
   chopped
2–3 garlic cloves,
   finely chopped
1 red pepper, diced
1 celery stalk, diced
1 x 14.5 oz
   chopped tomatoes
1 cup vegetable stock
1–2 handfuls of fresh
   baby leaf spinach
Small handful of
   mixed fresh herbs
Salt and black pepper,
   to taste
1¾ cups
   all-purpose flour
⅓ cup butter (or use
   vegan spread)
½ cup grated mature
   Cheddar (for a
   vegan version,
   omit the cheese
   or substitute with
   vegan cheese)

Vegetable Crumble

This is a very filling one-pot dish packed with goodness. Serve it on its own or with a salad for a perfect meal.

- Put the potatoes and carrots in a steamer and steam for 10 minutes to soften.
- Meanwhile, pour some olive oil in a skillet or frying pan and sauté the onions and garlic until they start to soften. Add the red pepper, celery, chopped tomatoes, vegetable stock, spinach, and herbs and cook for 10 minutes.
- Preheat the halogen oven using the preheat setting, or set the temperature to 350°F.
- Add the potatoes and carrots to the tomato mixture and season to taste. Pour this into an ovenproof dish.
- Put the flour into a bowl and use your fingers to rub in the butter to form a texture similar to bread crumbs. Add the grated cheese and season. Sprinkle this over the vegetable base.
- Place the crumble on the low rack and cook for 20 minutes until golden and bubbling. Serve immediately.

SUITABLE FOR VEGETARIANS OR VEGANS

Sausage and Mashed Vegetables

SERVES 4

With all the good vegetarian equivalents on the market these days, is no reason vegetarians can't enjoy traditional favorites, such as sausage.

- Preheat the halogen oven using the preheat setting, or set the temperature to 400°F.
- Put the potatoes, carrots, and sweet potatoes in a steamer and cook until soft and ready to mash.
- Meanwhile, drizzle some olive oil in the bottom of an ovenproof dish. Add the sausages, garlic, onion, and red currant jelly. Mix well.
- Place on the low rack and cook for 20 minutes. A couple of times during cooking, stir with a wooden spoon to combine the flavors.
- When the sausages have browned, add the wine and gravy or stock. Mix well. If the gravy needs thickening, pour a little water in a cup and add 1 teaspoon of cornstarch. Stir well, then add to the gravy, stirring until blended. Leave to thicken naturally for a few minutes.
- Put back in the oven for another 15 minutes.
- Mash the potatoes and vegetables together, adding a little butter or milk.
- Serve with green vegetables.

SUITABLE FOR VEGETARIANS AND VEGANS

4–5 potatoes, diced
2 carrots, diced
1 sweet potato, diced
Drizzle of olive oil
6–8 good-quality
  vegetarian sausages
1 garlic clove, crushed
1–2 red or Spanish
  onions, sliced
1 tablespoon red
  currant jelly
½ cup plus 2
  tablespoons red wine
1¼ cups gravy or
  stock, heated
2 tablespoons butter
  or ¼ cup milk
  (or use vegan spread
  or soy milk)

2 cups lentils

2 carrots, diced in
  small cubes

1 bay leaf

1–1½ cups water

Drizzle of olive oil

1 onion,
  finely chopped

2 garlic cloves,
  crushed

1 bell pepper, red or
  green, finely
  chopped

½ cup rolled oats

¼ cup cooked
  brown rice

1 teaspoon mixed
  herbs

Salt and black pepper,
  to taste

2–3 ripe tomatoes,
  chopped

1–2 teaspoons sun-dried
  tomato paste

Lentil Loaf

Traditionally, this loaf would have been used instead of meat to make up a vegetarian roast, but you can also slice it to accompany most meals. Serve with a creamy cheese sauce or, for a vegan version, opt for a herby tomato and basil sauce.

- Preheat the halogen oven using the preheat setting, or set the temperature to 350°F.
- Put the lentils, carrots, and bay leaf in a saucepan of water. Boil for 10 minutes, then drain and put in a bowl, reserving the water.
- Meanwhile, fry the onions in a little olive oil. Add the garlic and pepper. Once cooked, add to the bowl with the lentils and carrots.
- Add the remaining ingredients to form a thick mixture that is not too wet. Use the retained stock if the mixture is too dry.
- Pour into a well-greased or lined 1-lb loaf pan and bake on the low rack for 30 minutes.
- Let stand for 10 minutes before turning out onto a plate.

Note: For variation, put half the mixture in your loaf pan, add some cheese sauce or crumbled feta, mozzarella or even blue cheese. Put the remaining mixture over the cheese and press down firmly. Bake as above.

British Cheese Scones

MAKES 8–10 SCONES

I love cheese scones, especially when made with mature cheese, a touch of cayenne pepper, and paprika. Enjoy these hot or cold, but they're best eaten on the day they're made.

2 cups self-rising flour
1 teaspoon dry
   mustard
Pinch of cayenne
   pepper
Salt and black pepper,
   to taste
2 tablespoons butter
½ cup grated
   mature Cheddar
½ cup milk

- Preheat the halogen oven using the preheat setting, or set the temperature to 400°F.
- Sift the flour into a bowl. Add the cayenne pepper and mustard and season to taste.
- Add the butter and use your fingers to rub it in to form "bread crumbs." Add the grated cheese and mix well.
- Gradually add the milk to form a dough that is firm but not wet.
- Put the dough on a floured board, and press out to a 1¼–1½-inch thickness. Cut the scones out with a cookie cutter and place them on a greased baking sheet. Brush with milk.
- Place the scones in the halogen oven on the low rack and bake for 10 minutes. Once baked, put them on a cooling rack or serve warm.

Note: There's no reason why you can't add finely chopped onion. Non-vegetarians might like to try adding some chopped cooked bacon for a delicious savory scone. Experiment by adding your favorite herbs. You can also use this recipe to form a cobbler topping on a savory dish.

SUITABLE FOR VEGETARIANS

SERVES 4

Olive oil

1 onion, finely
   chopped

2–3 garlic cloves,
   crushed

1 red bell pepper,
   diced

6 Quorn fillets
   or pieces

¾ cup chopped
   button mushrooms

2 teaspoons paprika

1 x 14.5 oz can of
   chopped tomatoes

2 teaspoons sun-dried
   tomato paste

1 cup red wine

1 cup stock or water

1 cup whole
   button mushrooms

Small handful of fresh
   basil, chopped

Salt and black pepper,
   to taste

Quorn Italiano

This vegetarian variation of Chicken Italiano is delicious. Note:
Quorn is not suitable for vegans.

- In a large skillet or frying pan, fry the onions and
  garlic in a dash of olive oil for 2 minutes. Add the
  peppers and cook for another 2 minutes.
- Add the Quorn, mushrooms, and paprika. Stir,
  cooking gently for 5 minutes.
- Add all the remaining ingredients. Cook for another
  couple of minutes.
- Pour this into a casserole dish. Cover and cook at
  350°F for 30 minutes.
- Serve with small roast or sauté potatoes
  and vegetables.

SUITABLE FOR VEGETARIANS

Quorn and Mushroom Casserole

A wholesome meal that everyone loves. Note: Quorn is not suitable for Vegans

- 1 teaspoon dried tarragon (or a handful of fresh tarragon)
- Heat a little olive oil in a skillet or frying pan and cook the garlic, leeks, and scallions for 2–3 minutes. Add the Quorn and the mushrooms and cook for a further 5 minutes.
- Put the Quorn mixture in a casserole dish. Add the wine and stock.
- Mix the cornstarch with 2 teaspoons of water to form a smooth paste, then add this to the casserole.
- Add all the remaining ingredients. If using fresh tarragon, add half now and retain half to add in the last 10 minutes of cooking.
- Cook at 350°F for 30 minutes. If the casserole starts to form a skin on top, cover it, or wrap a piece of aluminum foil securely over the top.

SUITABLE FOR VEGETARIANS

A drizzle of olive oil
1–2 garlic cloves
2 leeks, finely chopped
6 scallions (spring onions), finely chopped
10 oz Quorn pieces
6 oz (about 2 cups) mushrooms, sliced
1 cup white wine
1¼ cups vegetable stock
1 teaspoon cornstarch
1 teaspoon paprika
¾ cup French beans

Desserts

Who can resist a delicious dessert to finish off a meal? In restaurants I have often been tempted to choose an appetizer and dessert and omit the main meal altogether.

Desserts don't always have to be calorie-laden feasts (although they're great occasionally!). In this chapter you'll find some desserts that are surprisingly good for you. My personal favorite is the Healthy Brûlèe, which literally takes minutes to make.

¾–1 cup strawberries,
quartered or
thickly sliced
8 oz cream cheese
5–6 oz Greek yogurt
2–3 tablespoons
crème fraîche or
sour cream
1 teaspoon
vanilla paste
Juice and zest of
1–2 lemons
6–8 graham crackers
2–3 tablespoons
brown sugar

Upside-down Strawberry Cheesecake

I'm a big fan of cheesecake and this is a tasty variation of the classic recipe.

- Put the strawberries in the bottom of an ovenproof serving dish that's big enough for 4–6 servings.
- Combine the cream cheese, yogurt, and crème fraîche. Add the vanilla paste and stir well.
- Roughly peel the lemon with a vegetable peeler to remove the rind. Chop this finely before adding to the cream cheese mixture. Also add the juice of the lemon. Taste and add another lemon if you prefer a more zesty flavor. When you're happy with the mix, carefully spoon it over the strawberries.
- Put the graham crackers in a bowl and use the end of a wooden rolling pin to crush them gently into crumbs.
- Sprinkle the crumbs over the cream cheese mixture and follow with a sprinkling of brown sugar.
- Put in the refrigerator for at least 30 minutes.
- Set the halogen oven to 475°F. Put the cheesecake on the high rack for 3 minutes, then serve.

Note: You can use frozen or fresh raspberries for the cheesecake. You could also try blueberries. If using frozen fruit, use the halogen's defrost setting and place the fruit in the ovenproof serving dish on the low rack for 10 minutes before adding the cream cheese mixture.

SUITABLE FOR VEGETARIANS

Baked Bananas
with Chocolate Sauce

SERVES 4

This is so simple but tastes amazing.

- Preheat the halogen oven using the preheat setting, or set the temperature to 350°F.
- Place the bananas in their skins on an ovenproof pan and bake on the low rack for 10 minutes, or until the skin goes completely black.
- Meanwhile, melt the chocolate, butter, honey, and cocoa powder in a bowl over a saucepan of water or use a double-boiler/bain marie.
- When ready to serve, pour the chocolate mixture over the bananas and finish with a generous scoop of ice-cream.

SUITABLE FOR VEGETARIANS

4 bananas
4-oz bar of
   dark chocolate
2 tablespoons butter
1–2 tablespoons honey
1 tablespoon
   cocoa powder

SERVES 4–6

4–6 ripe pears
1¾–2 cups
   mulled wine
1 orange, thickly sliced
¾ cup sugar

Mulled Baked Pears

This can be prepared in advance. Serve with vanilla ice-cream.

- Preheat your halogen oven using the preheat setting or set temperature to 325°F.
- Pour the wine in a saucepan and heat gently. Add half the sugar and stir until dissolved.
- Peel the pears retaining the stalk if possible. Cut the bottom off each pear to allow it to stand without falling over.
- Place the orange slices in the bottom of an ovenproof dish, (The smaller the dish, the more pear will be covered in wine).
- Place the pears in the dish, either on top of the orange slices or flat to allow more of the fruit to be covered in the liquid.
- Pour the wine over the pears. Sprinkle the pears with the remainder of the sugar.
- Cover securely with foil and bake on the low rack for 1 hour.
- Uncover and spoon the wine back over the pears. Add more wine if necessary.
- Cook uncovered for another 20 minutes, or until the pears are soft.
- Put the pears on a plate and drizzle over with the juice. Serve with ice cream or Greek yogurt.

SUITABLE FOR VEGETARIANS AND VEGANS

Baked Raspberry Cheesecake

SERVES 6

If you don't want raspberries, try other berries such as blueberry, or even raisins soaked in liqueur.

- In a bowl, cut the butter into small pieces. Add the flour and use your fingers to rub the butter pieces into it until the mixture resembles fine bread crumbs.
- Mix the sugar, egg yolks, and 2 tablespoons of water.
- Add this to the flour and mix to a soft dough. If necessary, add a tablespoon of water.
- Spread the mixture into a greased or lined springform pan, pressing down firmly. Sprinkle the raspberries on top.
- To make the topping, beat the egg whites until stiff, then add the sugar and beat for 1 minute.
- In a bowl, beat the cream cheese and vanilla, then fold in the egg whites.
- Spread the mixture over the raspberries. Place on the low rack in the halogen oven, turn the temperature to 350°F and bake for 35-45 minutes, or until firm and golden.
- Leave to cool and serve with a scattering of fresh raspberries as a garnish.

SUITABLE FOR VEGETARIANS

½ cup butter
2½ cups self-rising flour
½ cup superfine sugar
3 egg yolks
1 cup raspberries

For the topping
3 egg whites
¼ cup sugar
2 cups cream cheese
1 teaspoon vanilla extract or paste

SERVES 4-6

1¼ lb chopped fruit
(I use rhubarb,
apples, and plums,
or apple mixed with
frozen forest fruits)
½–⅔ cup red wine or
orange juice
½ cup sugar
3 teaspoons ground
cinnamon
1 teaspoon allspice
½ cup plus 2
tablespoons all-
purpose flour
½ cup rolled oats
1 teaspoon apple
pie spice
⅓ cup butter
(for a vegan version,
use dairy-free
margarine)
½ cup sliced almonds

Winter Spice Crumble

If you love the flavor of cinnamon and allspice, this is the pudding for you. Serve with vanilla ice-cream.

- Preheat the halogen oven using the preheat setting, or set the temperature to 350°F.
- Place the fruit in a saucepan and add the wine or orange juice and half of the sugar. Cook gently for 5–8 minutes to begin softening the fruit.
- Mix in the cinnamon and allspice and stir well, pressing the fruit a little with your spoon to help break and soften. Pour into an ovenproof dish.
- In a bowl, combine the flour, oats, and apple pie spice. Add the butter and rub it in with your fingers until the mixture resembles bread crumbs. Add the remaining sugar and almonds and mix well.
- Pour this over the fruit base, making sure it is spread evenly.
- Put the crumble on the low rack and bake for 20 minutes.
- Serve with vanilla ice-cream.

SUITABLE FOR VEGETARIANS AND VEGANS

Lemon Saucy Pudding

SERVES 4–6

- Using a food processor or cake mixer, beat the butter and sugar together until creamy.
- Using a sharp vegetable peeler, peel the zest from 2 or 3 lemons (depending on your desired lemony intensity). The peeler magically peels the zest and leaves the white pith behind. Finely chop the zest and add to the beaten sugar and butter mixture.
- Add the egg yolks, vanilla, and lemon juice. Beat well before adding the flour and milk. This will form quite a runny batter. Give it a thorough stir to make sure the mixer hasn't left anything on the edges of the bowl.
- Meanwhile, in a clean bowl, beat the egg whites until they form soft peaks. Fold gently into the batter.
- Grease a baking dish with butter. I use a Pyrex baking dish, but you could use individual ramekin dishes. Pour in the batter.
- Pour about an inch of hot water into your halogen oven, then place the baking dish in the water to create a bain marie. If you prefer (and have room), you can place a baking sheet filled with water on the lower rack and place the small ramekin dishes into it.
- Turn the halogen oven to 300°F and cook for 40–45 minutes (20–30 minutes if using individual ramekin dishes). The pudding should have a golden "sponge" topping that is firm to touch.
- Serve with crème fraîche or Greek yogurt. The bottom half of the pudding is a gooey lemon sauce and the top should be a light "sponge."

SUITABLE FOR VEGETARIANS

¼ cup butter
¾ cup sugar
Zest and juice of
   2 large or
   3 medium lemons
4 medium eggs (or 3 large), separated
1 teaspoon vanilla extract or paste
½ cup all-purpose flour
1¼ cups milk
2 teaspoons butter

SUITABLE FOR VEGETARIANS

Chocolate, Apple, and Hazelnut Betty

3 cooking apples, cored, peeled and sliced

2 tablespoons sugar

1–2 tablespoons water

2½ cups bread crumbs

½ cup rolled oats

⅓ cup chopped hazelnuts

½ cup dark chocolate chunks (for a vegan version, use dairy-free chocolate)

2 teaspoons ground cinnamon

½ cup butter (for a vegan version, use dairy-free margarine)

3 tablespoons light corn syrup

This is simply delicious!

- Preheat the halogen oven using the preheat setting, or set the temperature to 375°F.
- Place the apple slices in an ovenproof dish. Sprinkle with the sugar and water, then place on the low rack and cook for 10 minutes. Stir and cook for another 5 minutes before removing from the oven.
- While the apples are cooking, combine the bread crumbs, oats, hazelnuts, chocolate, and cinnamon. Put this mixture over the top of the fruit.
- Put the butter and syrup in an ovenproof dish and melt using the heat from the halogen oven—don't allow it to burn. Once melted, pour this mixture over the crumble mixture.
- Return the dish to the halogen and place on the low rack. Cook for another 15–20 minutes, or until the top is golden.
- Serve with crème fraîche or vanilla ice cream.

SUITABLE FOR VEGETARIANS AND VEGANS

Raspberry Healthy Brûlèe

SERVES 4-6

A really tasty dessert that takes minutes to prepare. This brûlèe looks and tastes far more impressive than it really is—and the good news is that it is actually very healthy! I make this in the same heatproof dish I serve it in, which is large enough for 4–6 portions. Alternatively use individual serving dishes such as ramekins; just make sure they're heatproof.

- If using frozen raspberries, put them in a heatproof dish and set it on the high rack for 10 minutes with the halogen oven set to thaw.
- Meanwhile, mix the yogurt and crème fraîche together in a bowl. Once combined, add the vanilla paste and stir well.
- Remove the raspberries from the halogen. If using a different serving dish, or ramekin dishes, put the raspberries in the bottom at this stage.
- Spoon the yogurt mixture over the berries, then add a sprinkling of brown sugar—enough to form a generous layer to make the crème brûlèe effect.
- Place back in the halogen oven on the high rack. Turn to the highest setting (usually 475°F) for 3–4 minutes, allowing the brown sugar to start to melt and caramelize. The beauty of the halogen is that you can see the dessert while it cooks—and therefore avoid letting it burn.
- Serve and enjoy!

SUITABLE FOR VEGETARIANS

1¾ cups frozen raspberries (or fresh)
1½–1¾ cups Greek yogurt
3 tablespoons low-fat crème fraîche (optional)
1 teaspoon vanilla paste
3–4 tablespoons brown sugar

½ cup sugar
½ cup butter
2 eggs, beaten
2 tablespoons milk
1 tablespoon vanilla
  extract or paste
1 cup self-rising flour
2 tablespoons
  cocoa powder
1¼ cups boiling water
2 tablespoons sugar
1 tablespoon
  cocoa powder

Chocolate Saucy Pudding

My mother used to make this when we were children, and I rediscovered the recipe when I borrowed her personal "oven notebook." We used to call this "magic pudding," because although the sauce is poured over the top of the cake, it miraculously goes to the bottom during baking. I've adapted it to suit the halogen and it works really well. You can make this in small ramekin dishes, but adjust the cooking time if you do.

• Preheat the halogen oven using the preheat setting, or set the temperature to 350°F.
• In a mixing bowl, beat the sugar and butter until creamy and fluffy. Gradually add the beaten eggs, milk, and vanilla, and mix well before adding the flour and cocoa powder.
• Pour this batter into a greased ovenproof dish (or ramekin dishes) and smooth over until flat.
• In a bowl, mix the boiling water, sugar, and cocoa powder together and stir thoroughly until lump-free. Pour this over the cake mixture.
• Place on the low rack and cook for 40–50 minutes, until the sponge layer is firm to touch.
• Serve with Greek yogurt or crème fraîche and enjoy!

SUITABLE FOR VEGETARIANS

Peach Melba Delight

SERVES 4–6

This is another favorite in our house. It's similar to Raspberry Healthy Brûlée on page 183. Use fresh peaches in season or, if you're in a hurry, try canned peaches in their own juice.

- Put the raspberries in an ovenproof dish and sprinkle with 1 tablespoon of sugar. Place on the low rack and cook for 5 minutes at 350°F to soften.
- Remove and crush. If you don't want seeds, put the berries through a strainer for a finer purée.
- In a bowl, mix the yogurt and crème fraîche with the vanilla paste.
- Place the sliced peaches in the bottom of an ovenproof serving dish. Drizzle with two-thirds of the raspberry purée.
- Add the raspberry purée to the yogurt and fold to create a ripple effect—don't over-stir.
- Pour this onto the peaches and smooth to form an even layer. Cover with a generous amount of brown sugar.
- Place on the high rack for 3–4 minutes at 475°F (or your highest setting). Watch it constantly, to prevent burning.
- Serve hot or cold.

SUITABLE FOR VEGETARIANS

2 cups raspberries
   (frozen or fresh)
4–5 tablespoons
   brown sugar
1½–1¾ cups
   Greek yogurt
3 tablespoons low-fat
   crème fraîche
   (optional)
1 teaspoon vanilla
   extract or paste
2–3 ripe peaches
   (or canned
   peaches), sliced

SERVES 4–6

4–5 cooking apples
1–2 tablespoons brown
  sugar (depending on
  desired sweetness)
1–2 teaspoons ground
  cinnamon
Juice of ½ a lemon
⅓ cup raisins
2 tablespoons water
1½ cups
  self-rising flour
2 level tablespoons
  of sugar
¼ cup butter
½ cup natural yogurt
1 teaspoon
  vanilla extract
Milk, to brush
A little extra brown
  sugar, to sprinkle

Apple and Cinnamon Cobbler

Apple and cinnamon are a bit like strawberries and cream—
they just fit together so well.

- Preheat the halogen oven using the preheat setting,
  or set the temperature to 400°F.
- Put the apples, brown sugar, cinnamon, lemon juice,
  and raisins in a saucepan. Add the water. Cook on
  medium heat until the apples start to soften, but not
  completely—you want them to retain some firmness.
- Meanwhile, sift the flour and put it with the sugar in a
  bowl. Use your fingers to rub the butter into the flour
  until the mixture resembles bread crumbs. Add the
  yogurt and vanilla and mix well.
- Turn out onto a floured surface and roll into a
  thick sausage shape, then use a cookie cutter to cut
  the dough into 1½–2-inch biscuit-like pieces.
- Pour the apple mixture into an ovenproof or
  casserole dish. Place the "biscuits" around the edge
  and on top of the apple mixture. Coat with a little
  milk and a sprinkle of brown sugar.
- Place on the low rack and cook for 15–18 minutes,
  until the cobbler pieces are golden.

SUITABLE FOR VEGETARIANS

Queen of Puddings

My mother used to make this for us when we were children. Comforting desserts are making a well-earned revival—they're so much nicer than shop-bought, processed varieties.

- Preheat the halogen oven using the preheat setting, or set the temperature to 350°F.
- Grease an ovenproof dish.
- Put the cubed bread in a bowl and sprinkle with the sugar.
- Heat the milk, vanilla extract, and butter to almost boiling point, then pour this over the bread and sugar mixture. When cool, add the egg yolks and whisk until smooth.
- Pour this into the ovenproof dish. Place on the low rack and cook for 30–35 minutes, or until set.
- Meanwhile, beat the egg whites until they form soft peaks, gradually adding half of the superfine sugar.
- Melt the jam on low heat (you don't want to burn it), then spread it over the set mixture. Top it with the whisked egg whites and sprinkle with the remaining superfine sugar.
- Place back in the oven and cook for another 8–10 minutes until golden.

SUITABLE FOR VEGETARIANS

Scant 1 up white
  bread cubes
¼ cup sugar
About 2 cups milk
1 teaspoon vanilla
  extract or paste
2½ tablespoons butter
2 eggs, separated
⅓ cup superfine sugar
3 tablespoons jam
  (I use raspberry, but
  feel free to use
  whatever you prefer)

SERVES 4–6

1¾ lb plums, halved,
   stones removed
1–2 tablespoons honey
A generous
   ⅓ cup of sugar
½ cup port
¼ cup water
confectioners sugar
   to sprinkle
Amaretti biscuits,
   to serve

Boozy Plums

A perfect dinner-party dessert. Make it as boozy as you like, but off set the alcoholic taste with some vanilla ice cream.

- Preheat the halogen oven using the preheat setting, or set the temperature to 300°F.
- Place the plums on a non-stick baking sheet or in an ovenproof dish.
- Drizzle the fruit with the honey and sprinkle it with a little sugar. Add the port and water before placing on the low rack and cooking for 30–40 minutes, or until the plums are soft.
- Remove and serve in individual bowls. Sprinkle with confectioners sugar and serve with some amaretti biscuits.

SUITABLE FOR VEGETARIANS

Apple and Date Bread-and-butter Pudding

A variation on a traditional favorite.

- Grease an ovenproof dish with butter. Butter the bread slices and line the dish, sprinkling dates, apple, sugar, and cinnamon between the slices.
- Mix the eggs, milk, and cream (if using) in a bowl. Pour this over the bread mixture, pushing the bread down into the liquid where necessary. Set aside for about 10 minutes to absorb the milk.
- Preheat the halogen oven using the preheat setting, or set the temperature to 375°F.
- Push the bread down into the liquid, sprinkle with more cinnamon if you like, and place the dish on the low rack of the halogen.
- Cook for 30 minutes until the top is golden and the base is almost set.

SUITABLE FOR VEGETARIANS

4–6 slices of white bread (stale is ideal)
2 tablespoons butter
$\frac{1}{3}$ cup chopped dates
1 cooking apple, peeled and chopped
$\frac{1}{4}$ cup sugar
2 teaspoons ground cinnamon
2 eggs, beaten
$1\frac{1}{4}$ cups milk
$\frac{1}{4}$ cup cream (optional—instead you can increase the milk to $1\frac{1}{2}$ cups)

For the pastry

1½ cups all-purpose
   flour

½ cup butter

⅓ cup plus 1
   tablespoon sugar

1 egg, beaten

1 tablespoon water

2¼ lb cooking apples

Squeeze of
   lemon juice

1 tablespoon butter

⅓ cup sugar

1–2 teaspoons
   cinnamon

3 tablespoons
   apricot jam

French Apple Tart

This is a lovely dish. The recipe includes the process for making the pastry shell but, if you aren't up to making your own, use a bought equivalent.

- To make the pastry, put the flour in a bowl. Add the butter and use your fingers to rub it into the flour until the mixture resembles fine bread crumbs.
- Add the sugar and mix well. Add the beaten egg and water and combine to form a dough. Place the dough in the refrigerator to rest while you continue with the rest of the recipe.
- Peel and thinly slice the apples and cover them with water and a squeeze of lemon juice.
- Preheat the halogen oven using the preheat setting, or set the temperature to 400°F.
- Roll out the pastry and line a pie plate, first making sure it fits in the halogen oven. Prick the pastry with a fork, cover it with a sheet of parchment paper, and put pie weights or dried beans on the paper; bake it on the low rack for 15 minutes to bake blind.
- Meanwhile, remove a third of the apple slices and place them in a pan to soften with a little butter, a drizzle of water, and the sugar. Stir until soft before adding almost all the cinnamon.
- Remove the pastry shell, take off the paper and weights or beans, and spoon in the puréed apple.

Smooth the top, then add the apple slices in a nice even pattern, fanning them out and overlapping slightly around the pie plate. Sprinkle with sugar and the remaining cinnamon.

• Return to the low rack and bake for 25 minutes, or until the apples are cooked. Remove from the oven and set aside.

• Gently heat the apricot jam in a saucepan, stirring continuously to avoid burning. Once the jam is runny, brush it over the baked apple, ensuring the top is well covered.

• Serve hot or cold with ice cream or just by itself.

SUITABLE FOR VEGETARIANS

Pineapple Upside-down Cake

SERVES 4–6

½ cup plus 2
   tablespoons butter
¾ cup sugar
3 eggs, beaten
1½ cups self-rising
   flour, sifted
1 teaspoon vanilla
   extract
¼ cup butter
¼ cup brown sugar
2 tablespoons light
   corn syrup
6 pineapple rings
   (from canned
   pineapple)
3 maraschino
   cherries, halved

A traditional family favorite that can be used as a dessert at the end of a meal, or simply as a cake for any time.

- In a mixing bowl, beat the butter and sugar until golden and creamy.
- Gradually add the eggs and mix well.
- Fold in the sifted flour and, once combined thoroughly, add the vanilla extract.
- Preheat the halogen oven using the preheat setting, or set the temperature to 350°F.
- Place ¼ cup of butter, the brown sugar, and corn syrup in an ovenproof bowl. Using the preheat temperature, melt the butter, but don't let it burn.
- Grease or line an ovenproof dish or 8–9-inch cake pan thoroughly.
- Put a small amount of the butter and sugar mixture into the dish, then place the pineapples in the bottom with a cherry half in the middle of each pineapple ring. Add the remaining melted butter and sugar.

- Carefully spoon on the cake batter, covering the pineapple rings. Once completely covered, carefully smooth over the surface.
- Place on the low rack and cook until the cake has risen, is golden, and springs back into shape when touched—this should take between 25–30 minutes.
- Remove from the oven. Place a plate or serving dish over the top of the pan and flip it over so that the cake sits on the plate, upside down, pineapple facing upwards.

SUITABLE FOR VEGETARIANS

2–3 cooking apples,
  cored, peeled and
  sliced
10 oz (about 2 cups)
  mixed frozen berries
1–2 tablespoons sugar
1–2 tablespoons water
2½ cups bread crumbs
½ cup rolled oats
2 teaspoons cinnamon
½ cup butter (for the
  vegan version, use
  dairy-free
  margarine)
3 tablespoons light
  corn syrup

Fruit Berry Betty

Fill this wonderful dessert with a mixture of fruit and berries for a great burst of vitamin C, zing, and flavors. A great variation to the standard British fruit crumble.

- Preheat the halogen oven using the preheat setting, or set the temperature to 375°F.
- Put the apple and berries in an ovenproof dish. Sprinkle with the sugar and water.
- Place on the low rack and cook for 10 minutes. Stir and cook for another 5 minutes before removing from the oven.
- While the apple and berries are cooking, combine the bread crumbs, oats, and cinnamon. Spoon this mixture over the top of the fruit.
- Put the butter and syrup in an ovenproof dish and melt using the heat from the halogen oven—do not allow it to burn. Once melted, pour it over the crumble mixture.
- Return the dish to the halogen and place it on the low rack. Bake for another 15–20 minutes, or until the top is golden.
- Serve with vanilla ice cream.

SUITABLE FOR VEGETARIANS AND VEGANS

Roasted Plums

SERVES 4–6

It is not just vegetables that can be roasted. Plums are delicious when slow-cooked—they're perfect for the halogen.

- Preheat the halogen oven using the preheat setting, or set the temperature to 350°F.
- Wash the plums. While they are still wet, roll them in sugar, then place them on a greased or buttered baking sheet, or greased ovenproof dish.
  Add the water.
- Put on the low rack and cook for 10 minutes.
- Drizzle honey over the plums and sprinkle them with cinnamon before cooking again for another 10–15 minutes, or until they are cooked.
- Serve with crème fraîche or ice cream.

SUITABLE FOR VEGETARIANS

8–12 plums
Sugar
2–3 tablespoons water
1–2 tablespoons
   of honey
Ground cinnamon

For the pastry

1½ cup all-purpose flour

⅓ cup butter

⅓ cup plus 2 teaspoons sugar

1 egg, beaten

1 tablespoon water

For the filling

½ cup butter

⅔ cup sugar

2 eggs

1 cup ground almonds

1 tablespoon all-purpose flour

1–2 teaspoons cinnamon

2 apples, sliced

½ cup blackberries

2 tablespoons apricot jam

Apple and Blackberry Frangipane Tart

I love the look of this tart almost as much as the taste. Sprinkle with confectioners sugar before serving. Delicious hot or cold.

- To make the pastry, put the flour in a bowl. Use your fingers to rub the butter into the flour, until it forms a mixture that resembles fine bread crumbs.
- Add the sugar and mix well. Add the beaten egg and water and combine to form a dough. Put the dough in the refrigerator to rest while you continue with the rest of the recipe.
- Preheat the halogen oven using the preheat setting, or set the temperature to 400°F.
- Roll out the pastry and line a pie plate. Prick the pastry with a fork, cover it with a sheet of parchment paper, and put pie weights or baking beans on top of the paper. Place on the low rack of the oven for 15 minutes to bake blind.
- While the pastry is baking, beat the butter and sugar in a mixing bowl until light and fluffy. Gradually add the eggs. When this is well beaten, add the ground almonds, flour, and cinnamon. Beat well.
- Pour this mixture onto the pastry shell. Over the top, place the apple slices in a nice even pattern around the pie plate. Add the blackberries in between the apple slices and press into the sponge mixture.
- Return to the low rack and bake for 25–30 minutes until the apples are cooked and the cakee has risen. Remove from the oven.

- Gently heat the apricot jam in a saucepan on your stove top, stirring continuously to avoid it burning. Once the jam is runny, brush it over the baked apples, ensuring the top is well covered and has a glaze. Return the tart to the halogen for 5 more minutes.
- Serve hot or cold with ice cream—or just on its own.

SUITABLE FOR VEGETARIANS

SERVES 4–6

1 lb 9 oz cooking
 apples, cored,
 peeled and diced
2 tablespoons water
¼ cup brown sugar
⅓ cup raisins
1 teaspoon cinnamon
1 small ginger
 cake, crumbled
Juice and zest of
 1 orange
1 tablespoon
 unsweetened
 coconut flakes
1 tablespoon
 brown sugar

Quick Ginger-Apple Layer

This is such a simple dish, made using some pantry staples.
It can be thrown together in minutes—perfect for a quick and
easy dessert.

- Put the chopped apples in a saucepan and add the
  water and sugar. Cook until the fruit starts to soften,
  but still has a bite (i.e. don't purée it). Add the raisins
  and cinnamon and mix well.
- Preheat the halogen oven using the preheat setting,
  or set the temperature to 350°F.
- Grease an ovenproof dish.
- Crumble a layer of ginger cake in the bottom of the
  dish. Over this, add a layer of apple. Repeat, finishing
  with a ginger cake top layer.
- Pour the orange juice and zest over the cake, then
  sprinkle with the coconut and brown sugar.
- Place on the low rack and cook for 15–20 minutes.
- Serve with Homemade Custard (see page 200) or
  Butterscotch Sauce (see the next recipe). Delicious!

SUITABLE FOR VEGETARIANS

Butterscotch Sauce

- Put the butter, brown sugar, and light corn syrup in an ovenproof bowl (or saucepan if you prefer not to use the halogen oven). Melt together gently but don't let it burn. Stir well to combine.
- Fold in the cream.
- Serve hot or cold.

SUITABLE FOR VEGETARIANS

¼ cup butter
⅔ cup brown sugar
6 tablespoons light
  corn syrup
6 tablespoons
  heavy cream

2½ cups whole milk

4 egg yolks

4 tablespoons
   cornstarch

3 tablespoons sugar

1 teaspoon
   vanilla extract

Homemade Custard

• Heat the milk until just below boiling point.
• While it heats, mix the egg yolks, cornstarch, and
   sugar in a bowl.
• Remove the milk from the heat and add the egg
   mixture to it. Use a whisk and stir well.
• Place back on the heat and continue to stir until the
   custard starts to thicken—be careful not to have the
   heat up too high or it will burn.
• Once the custard has reached your desired thickness,
   remove it from the heat. Serve immediately.

Note: If you have any custard left over, pour it into
popsicle molds and freeze. Delicious!

SUITABLE FOR VEGETARIANS

Pear and Chocolate Granola Layer

You can mix granola with semi-sweet chocolate chips. This dessert is excellent served hot or cold.

- Put the pears in a saucepan, add the water and cook until they start to soften. Once the fruit has softened, stir in the sugar.
- Preheat the halogen oven using the preheat setting, or set the temperature to 350°F.
- In a bowl, mix the granola, chocolate chips, and hazelnuts.
- Spoon half the pears into an ovenproof dish. Cover with a layer of granola. Add the final layer of pears and cover again with the granola.
- Place in the oven on the low rack and bake for 15 minutes.
- Serve hot or cold.

SUITABLE FOR VEGETARIANS

8 ripe pears, peeled, cored, and diced
2 tablespoons water
1 tablespoon sugar
8–12 tablespoons granola
Generous ½ cup semi-sweet chocolate chips
2 tablespoons chopped hazelnuts

Cakes and Treats

Most people worry about using the halogen oven to bake cakes. Many believe cakes will burn on top and remain uncooked in the middle, but don't panic: this only happens if you have the temperature set too high. Remember, the halogen oven comes with a powerful fan that helps distribute the heat around the bowl evenly.

Chocolate Chip Cupcakes with Vanilla Butter Icing

MAKES 8–12

½ cup cocoa powder
1 tablespoon
   boiling water
1¾ cups butter
1¾ cups sugar
3 eggs, beaten
1¾ cups
   self-rising flour
⅓ cups semi-sweet
   chocolate chips

Vanilla Butter Icing
2 tablespoons butter
½ cup cream cheese
1¾–2 cups
   confectioners sugar
1 teaspoon vanilla
   extract or paste
Chocolate chips or
   grated chocolate,
   to sprinkle

- Preheat the halogen oven using the preheat setting, or set to 400°F.
- Mix the cocoa powder with the hot water and set aside.
- In a mixing bowl, cream the butter and sugar together until pale and fluffy. Add the eggs a little at a time and continue to beat well.
- Sift the flour and fold it into the mixture gently.
- When thoroughly mixed, add the cocoa mixture and chocolate chips and stir well.
- Spoon into cupcake or muffin cases in a round muffin or cupcake pan. I haven't been able to find a round muffin tray so I use silicon muffin cases and place them on the halogen baking sheets that come with the accessory packs. You can comfortably fit 10 on the sheet.
- Place on the low rack and cook for 12–15 minutes. The cupcakes should be firm and spring back when touched. Once cooked, place them on a coolin rack to cool.
- While the cupcakes are cooling, make the icing. Beat the butter and cream cheese together until soft.
- Gradually add the confectioners sugar and vanilla extract and beat until you reach the desired consistency—it should be glossy, thick, and lump-free. The best way of testing to see if you have added enough confectioners sugar is to taste it. It should taste sweet and creamy but not too buttery.

- If you're using silicon muffin cases, wait until the cupcakes are completely cool, then carefully pull away the sides of each case. Once the case is clear all the way around, turn it upside down and the cupcake should pop out.
- Put the icing into an icing bag. Start in the center of each cupcake and spiral outwards, covering the whole of the cupcake top, gently overlapping to avoid gaps.
- Finish with a sprinkle of a few chocolate chips or grated chocolate and you're ready to serve.

SUITABLE FOR VEGETARIANS

British Fruit Scones

MAKES 8–10

2 cups self-rising flour
2 tablespoons butter
2 tablespoons sugar
⅓ cup raisins
½ cup milk

- Preheat the halogen oven to 400°F.
- Sift the flour into a bowl. Add the butter and use your fingers to rub it into the flour until the mixture resembles fine bread crumbs. Add the sugar and dried fruit and mix well.
- Gradually add the milk to form a dough that is firm but not wet.
- Turn out the dough onto a floured board and press out into a 1¼–½-inch thickness. Cut out the scones with a cookie cutter and place them on a greased baking sheet. Brush with milk.
- Place in the halogen oven on the low rack for 10–12 minutes.
- When baked, place on a cooling rack.
- Serve with cream and jam for a traditional British cream tea.

SUITABLE FOR VEGETARIANS

Fruit and Tea Loaf

This is another old British recipe, which I've slightly adapted. It is really easy to make.

- Make 1 cup of tea and leave it to steep for 5 minutes.
- Meanwhile, in a large saucepan, add the dried fruit, butter, and sugar. Then add the tea when it's ready.
- Put in a saucepan on moderate heat and gently allow the butter to melt and the sugar to dissolve. Keep stirring; you don't want this to stick or burn. Once the butter has melted, add the spices. Boil for 1 minute, then remove from the heat.
- Using sharp scissors, snip the apple rings into pieces and drop them into the saucepan. Stir well and leave until cold—or overnight if you prefer.
- Once the tea mixture has cooled and been absorbed, sift in the flour and stir well until thoroughly combined.
- Preheat the halogen oven using the preheat setting, or set the temperature to 350°F.
- Thoroughly grease or line a loaf pan and pour in the batter.
- Place on the low rack and bake for 20 minutes. Check the cake; if the top is getting too dark, cover with some parchment paper or aluminum foil—but make sure it is secure without restricting the cake.
- Turn down the temperature to 325°F and bake for another 25–30 minutes, or until a skewer, when inserted into the center of the cake, comes out clean.
- Leave the loaf to cool in the cake pan before turning it out onto a cooling rack.

MAKES APPROXIMATELY 8 SLICES

1 cup strong black tea
10 oz mixed dried fruit
½ cup butter (for a vegan version, use dairy-free margarine)
⅔ cup brown sugar
2 teaspoons ground cinnamon
1 teaspoon allspice
½ cup dried apple rings
2¼ cups self-rising flour

SUITABLE FOR VEGETARIANS AND VEGANS

MAKES 8–12

1¾ cups butter
¾ cup sugar
3 large eggs, beaten
1¾ cups
　self-rising flour
¾ cup raisins
2 tablespoons
　lemon curd
Juice and zest of
　1 lemon for topping
½ cup plus 2
　tablespoons sugar,
　for topping

SUITABLE FOR VEGETARIANS

Lemon Cupcakes

This is one of my mother's favorite recipes. The cupcakes are ideal for packed lunches, but beware: they might not last that long! They are delicious eaten warm!

- Preheat the halogen oven using the preheat setting, or set the temperature to 400°F.
- In a mixing bowl, cream the butter and sugar together until pale and fluffy. Add the eggs a little at a time and continue to beat well.
- Sift the flour and fold it into the mixture gently. When thoroughly mixed, roughly fold in the raisins and lemon curd. Don't over-fold; you want the lemon curd to have a "ripple effect."
- Spoon the mixture into cupcake or muffin cases in a muffin or cupcake pan. I haven't been able to find a round muffin tray, so I use silicon muffin cases and place them on the halogen baking sheets that come with the accessory packs. You can comfortably fit 10 on the sheet.
- Place on the low rack and bake for 12–15 minutes. The cupcakes should be firm and spring back when touched.
- While the cakes are cooking, juice and zest 1 lemon, then mix the juice and zest together. Once the cakes are cooked and still hot, pour a little of the lemon mix over each one and finish with a sprinkle of sugar.
- If using silicon muffin cases, wait until the cupcakes are cool, then carefully pull away the sides of each case. Once clear all the way around, turn each case upside down and the cupcake should pop out.

Cappuccino Cupcakes

MAKES 8–12

- Preheat the halogen oven using the preheat setting, or set the temperature to 400°F.
- Cream the butter and sugar together until pale and fluffy. Add the eggs a little at a time and continue to beat well.
- Sift the flour and fold it into the mixture gently. When thoroughly mixed, add the coffee essence and combine.
- Spoon the mixture into cupcake or muffin cases in a muffin pan. I use silicon muffin cases and put them on the halogen baking sheets that come with the accessory packs. You can fit 10 on the sheet.
- Put on the low rack and bake for 12–15 minutes. The cupcakes should be firm and spring back when touched.
- While the cupcakes cool on a cooling rack, make the icing. Beat the butter and cream cheese together until soft. Gradually add the confectioners sugar and vanilla extract and beat until you reach the desired consistency—it should be glossy, thick, and lump-free. The best way to test whether you've added enough confectioners sugar is to taste. The icing should taste sweet and creamy but not too buttery.
- If using silicon muffin cases, wait until the cupcakes are cool, then carefully pull away the sides of each case. Once a case is clear all the way around, turn it upside down and the cupcake should pop out.
- Put the icing into a icing bag. Start in the center of each cupcake and spiral outwards, covering the whole of the top, gently overlapping to avoid gaps. Finish with a sprinkle of cocoa powder to give a cappuccino effect, and you're ready to serve.

1¾ cups butter
1¾ cups sugar
3 eggs, beaten
1¾ cups
  self-rising flour
2–4 teaspoons coffee
  essence, depending
  on desired strength

Vanilla Butter Icing
2 tablespoons butter
½ cup cream cheese
2–2¾ cups
  confectioners sugar
1 teaspoon vanilla
  extract or paste
Cocoa powder,
  to sprinkle

SUITABLE FOR VEGETARIANS

1¾ cups butter
1¾ cups sugar
3 eggs, beaten
2 cups self-rising flour
Juice and zest of
  2 lemons

Icing
2 tablespoons butter
½ cup cream cheese
2½ cups confectioners
  sugar
Zest of 1 lemon
Slices of lemon,
  to garnish

Lemon Cream Cake

This delicious sponge cake has a lemon-cream filling. If you prefer, you can also put lemon cream all over the cake for a really decadent dessert.

- Preheat the halogen oven using the preheat setting, or set the temperature to 350°F.
- Cream the butter and sugar together until pale and fluffy. Add the eggs a little at a time and continue to beat well.
- Sift the flour and fold it into the mixture gently. When thoroughly mixed, add the juice and zest of the lemons and combine. For an extra lemon tang you could add a little lemon essence, but buy a good-quality one or it can taste too artificial.
- Pour the batter into 2 greased 8-inch cake pans.
- Turn the halogen oven down to 325°F, with the fan on full (if applicable).
- If you have an extension ring, bake the layers together. If you don't, I advise baking them on the low rack one at a time. If you use an extension ring, place one pan on the low rack and one on the high rack, but keep an eye on the top one. You may want to swap them over halfway through; otherwise the top layer may be ready a few minutes before the lower one.
- Bake for 25–35 minutes until firm to the touch and the cake has pulled away slightly from the edges of the pan.

- While the cakes are cooling, prepare the icing. Beat the butter and cream cheese together until soft. Gradually add the confectioners sugar and vanilla extract and beat until you reach the desired consistency—it should be glossy, thick, and lump-free. The best way of testing the icing to see if you've added enough confectioners sugar is to taste it. It should taste sweet and creamy but not too buttery.
- Spread the icing on one of the layers, then sandwich them together. For an extra touch of lemon, spread with lemon curd, then spread on the butter icing before sandwiching together.
- If you prefer, spread icing on the top, around the sides, or all over the cake. Finish with a couple of slices of lemon for decoration.

SUITABLE FOR VEGETARIANS

Blueberry Muffins

MAKES 8–12

1 cup light
  brown sugar
2 eggs, beaten
1 cup natural yogurt
1 teaspoon
  vanilla extract
3 cups self-rising flour
1¾ cups blueberries

- Preheat the halogen oven using the preheat setting, or set the temperature to 375°F.
- Beat the sugar and eggs in a bowl until fluffy. Add the yogurt and vanilla extract and beat again.
- Sift the flour into the mixture and carefully fold it in. When thoroughly mixed, add the blueberries.
- Spoon the batter into muffin cases in a muffin pan. I haven't been able to find a round muffin pan, so I use silicon muffin cases and place them on the halogen baking sheets that come with the accessory packs. You can comfortably fit 10 on the tray.
- Put the muffins on the low rack and bake for 12–15 minutes. The muffins should be firm and spring back when touched.
- Place onto a cooling rack before serving.

SUITABLE FOR VEGETARIANS

Upside-down Blackberry and Apple Cake

A springform cake pan is ideal for baking this cake.

- Preheat the halogen oven using the preheat setting, or set the temperature to 375°F.
- Generously grease an 8-inch cake pan with butter.
- Place the apple slices, blackberries, and 1 tablespoon of sugar in the base of the cake pan.
- In a mixing bowl, beat the butter and sugar until light and fluffy. Add the eggs a little at a time, and then add the sifted flour. Once mixed, add the vanilla extract and cinnamon. Mix well.
- Pour the cake batter over the apple and blackberries. Smooth the surface gently.
- Place on the low rack and bake for 30–40 minutes, until the cake is cooked, firm, and springs back to shape when touched.
- When ready to serve, place an upturned plate on the top of the cake pan. Flip it over so that the cake pan is upside down on top of the plate, then allow the cake to drop onto the plate. If using a springform cake pan, undo it to release the cake.
- Sprinkle with sifted confectioners sugar to decorate before serving hot or cold.

SUITABLE FOR VEGETARIANS

MAKES APPROXIMATELY 8 PIECES

2–3 cooking
   apples, sliced
1½ cups blackberries
1 tablespoon sugar
1¾ cups butter
1¾ cups sugar
3 eggs
1¾ cups self-rising flour
1 teaspoon
   vanilla extract
2 teaspoons cinnamon
Confectioners sugar,
   to serve

Aunt Ruth's Fabulous Ginger Cake

MAKES APPROXIMATELY 8 PIECES

½ teaspoon baking soda

4 tablespoons milk

½ cup butter

Generous ½ cup moist
  brown sugar

½ cup plus 2
  tablespoons molasses

2½ cups
  all-purpose flour

2 teapoons ginger

1 teaspoon grated
  lemon rind

1 egg

Candied ginger,
  to serve

When I was growing up, a visit to Aunt Ruth's house meant afternoon tea with delicious cakes. Here is one of her great recipes—I hope you enjoy it.

- Preheat the halogen oven using the preheat setting, or set the temperature to 300°F.
- Blend the baking soda with 1 tablespoon of milk.
- Put the butter, sugar, and syrup in a saucepan and heat until the butter has melted. Add the milk and heat gently.
- Sift the flour and ginger together in a bowl. Add the melted butter and syrup mixture, along with the milk and baking soda mixture, lemon rind, and egg. Whisk until well combined.
- Thoroughly grease or line an 8-inch cake pan or loaf pan. Pour in the mixture and bake on the low rack for 1 hour, 10 minutes–1 hour, 30 minutes. To check that it's done, gently press the center of the cake; if no impression is left, then it's ready.
- Leave the cake in the pan until cool, then turn it out onto a cooling rack.
- Serve iced or topped with sliced candied ginger.

SUITABLE FOR VEGETARIANS

Chocolate and Date Fingers

This chocolat snack is highly addictive. All you need is a cup of tea, a good book, and a comfortable sofa to go with it. Life can't get any better!

- Preheat the halogen oven using the preheat setting, or set the temperature to 350°F.
- In a saucepan, melt the chocolate, butter, sugar, and syrup on a low-medium heat, making sure it doesn't burn. Stir continuously.
- Add the chopped dates and the oats. Mix well.
- Pour into a greased pan or ovenproof dish. Press down gently.
- Place on the low rack and cook for 20–25 minutes.
- Leave in the pan to cool. Once cooled, cut into fingers.

SUITABLE FOR VEGETARIANS AND VEGANS

⅓ cup semi-sweet chocolate (for the vegan version, use dairy-free chocolate)
¾ cup butter (for the vegan version, use dairy-free margarine)
⅓ cup brown sugar
1 tablespoon light corn syrup
⅔ cup dates, roughly chopped
2½ cups rolled oats

MAKES 4–6

About ½ package of
    ready-to-bake
    puff pastry
Mincemeat (bought,
    use only as much
    as you need)d
2 tablespoons
    melted butter
Sprinkling of
    brown sugar

Simple Eccles Cakes

These British pastries were my dad's favorites when I was growing up. We children thought they were packed with dead flies(!), but I've matured since then and discovered that I really love them. They don't last long in our home, so here's a very fast and easy recipe to suit the craving.

- Preheat the halogen oven using the preheat setting, or turn the temperature to 400°F.
- Roll out the puff pastry to about 1½–2 inches thick. Cut into squares, approximately 6–8 inches square.
- Place 2–3 teaspoons of mincemeat in the center of each puff pastry square.
- Using a pastry brush, brush melted butter around the edges of the square. I normally fold the pastry diagonally, bringing each corner to the center to form an envelope or parcel. Alternatively, simply fold the pastry over and secure, either to form a rectangle or a triangle.
- On a floured surface, turn the cakes over so that the seam is on the bottom. Apply a bit of pressure on your rolling pin, or use your fingers, and gently roll the cakes flat, being careful not to split the pastry.
- Using a sharp knife, score 2 or 3 slits in the top of each cake. Brush with butter and sprinkle with brown sugar before placing on a greased baking sheet.
- Place on the low rack and bake for 15–18 minutes until golden.

SUITABLE FOR VEGETARIANS

Jam Turnovers

If I'm making some Eccles Cakes, my youngest son usually demands to help and inevitably wants to make Jam Turnovers. The recipe is similar to the Eccles recipe opposite, so I suggest making both to save time and money.

- Preheat the halogen oven using the preheat setting, or turn the temperature to 400°F.
- Roll out the puff pastry to about 1½–2 inches thick. Cut into squares, approximately 6–8 inches square.
- Place 2–3 teaspoons of jam in the center of each puff pastry square.
- Using a pastry brush, brush milk or egg around the edges of each square. I normally fold the pastry diagonally to form a triangle. Secure the edges by crimping.
- Brush with butter and a sprinkle of brown sugar before placing on a greased baking sheet.
- Place on the low rack and bake for 15–18 minutes until golden.

SUITABLE FOR VEGETARIANS

MAKES 4–6

About ½ package of
  ready-to-bake
  puff pastry
Jam of your choice
A little milk or
  beaten egg
A little butter, melted
Brown sugar,
  to sprinkle

Apple Turnovers

SERVES 4–6

About ½ package of
  ready-to-bake
  puff pastry
Stewed apples or
  2 cooking apples,
  cut into fine slices
Beaten egg or milk
Brown sugar,
  to sprinkle
Ground cinnamon to
  taste (optional)

These are great if you have any leftover puff pastry or stewed apples to use up. Stewed apples are easier, but you can also simply slice some cooking apples into the center of the pastry and add some sugar.

- Preheat the halogen oven using the preheat setting, or set the temperature to 400°F.
- Roll out the puff pastry to about 1½–2 inches thick. Cut into squares, approximately 6–8 inches square.
- Place 2–3 teaspoons of stewed apple or apple slices in the center of the puff pastry squares. If using apple slices, add a sprinkle of sugar and cinnamon to taste.
- Using a pastry brush, brush the milk or egg around the edges of each square. I normally fold the pastry diagonally to form a triangle. Secure the edges by crimping.
- Brush with butter and a sprinkle of brown sugar before placing on a greased baking sheet.
- Place on the low rack and bake for 15–18 minutes until golden.

SUITABLE FOR VEGETARIANS

Banana and Chocolate Cake

MAKES APPROXIMATELY 8 PIECES

- Preheat the halogen oven using the preheat setting, or set the temperature to 375°F.
- Using a cake mixer, beat the sugar and butter together in a bowl until light and fluffy. Add the honey, vanilla extract, and eggs and mix again.
- Add the banana. Sift the flour and cocoa powder together, then add this. Mix well.
- Pour into a well-greased or lined 8-inch cake pan (or a loaf pan) and bake on the low rack for 30 minutes, or until a skewer comes out clean when pushed into the center of the cake.
- Remove from the halogen and leave to cool slightly before turning out onto a cooling rack.
- Decorate with melted chocolate or Vanilla Butter Icing (see page 204 or 209).

SUITABLE FOR VEGETARIANS

½ cup sugar
½ cup butter
2 tablespoons honey
1 teaspoon vanilla extract
2 eggs, beaten
1 ripe banana, mashed
1½ cups self-rising flour
4 tablespoons cocoa powd

MAKES 8–10

2 tablespoons butter

1½ cups rolled oats

2 tablespoons
  brown sugar

3 tablespoons
  all-purpose flour

⅓ cup plus 1
  tablespoon sugar

1 egg, beaten

2 tablespoons
  natural yogurt

1 teaspoon
  vanilla extract

½ cup self-rising flour

⅔ cup chopped dates

⅓ cup chopped
  walnuts

Extra brown sugar,
  to sprinkle

Date and Walnut Slice

This is a really nice, healthy alternative to a cake. For added indulgence, add a handful of chocolate chips.

- Heat the butter in a saucepan or in a bowl in the halogen oven (just make sure it doesn't burn). Once melted, remove from the heat and stir in the oats, brown sugar, and flour.
- Press onto a lined baking sheet to form the base of the slices.
- Preheat the halogen oven using the preheat setting, or set the temperature to 350°F.
- While the oven is heating, beat the sugar and egg together in a bowl. Once light and fluffy, add the yogurt and vanilla extract.
- Add the flour, dates, and most of the walnuts, retaining a few to use on the top of the slices. Pour this mixture on top of the base. Spread it to cover the base and sprinkle with the remaining walnuts and a little brown sugar.
- Place on the low rack and cook for 20 minutes.
- Leave to cool for 5–10 minutes before slicing.

SUITABLE FOR VEGETARIANS

Viennese Whirls

MAKES 18–22 BISCUITS

When I was a teenager, my mother and I used to catch a bus to Exeter to go shopping and generally spend a girlie day together. On the way home we always bought a package of Viennese whirls and, before we got home, the package would be empty. Not much has changed since then; I can still demolish a whole portion of these delicious cookies! For this recipe you need to use good-quality butter because margarine doesn't really produce the same taste—or result.

¾ cup butter
½ cup
   confectioners sugar
½ teaspoon
   vanilla paste
1½ cups all-purpose
   flour, sifted
½ cup cornstarch, sifted

- Preheat the halogen oven using the preheat setting, or set the temperature to 400°F.
- Beat the butter, confectioners sugar, and vanilla paste together until light and fluffy.
- Gradually add the sifted flour and cornstarch until you have a firm but squeezable paste.
- Put this into a icing bag and make swirled cookes. If you don't want to mess around with icing bags, carefully drop spoonfuls onto a greased baking sheet. Make sure this tray fits well in your halogen oven— you'll probably need to bake it in two batches.
- Place on the low rack. (If you have an extension ring, bake both batches at the same time, but watch the top layer: cookies here will bake faster than those on the bottom.) Bake for 10–15 minutes, or until golden.
- Place on a cooling rack before enjoying. Store in an airtight container.

SUITABLE FOR VEGETARIANS

Carrot Cake Muffins with Vanilla Butter Icing

MAKES 8–12

1¾ cups butter
1 cup brown sugar
3 eggs, beaten
1¾ cups
  self-rising flour
2 teaspoons cinnamon
1 teaspoon coriander
2 carrots, grated
⅔ cup unsweetened
  coconut flakes

Vanilla Butter Icing
2 tablespoons butter
½ cup cream cheese
1¾–2 cups
  confectioners sugar
1 teaspoon vanilla
  extract or paste

- Preheat the halogen oven using the preheat setting, or set the temperature to 400°F.
- Cream the butter and sugar together until pale and fluffy. Add the eggs a little at a time and continue to beat well. Sift the flour and fold into the mixture gently.
- When thoroughly mixed, add the cinnamon, coriander, carrots, and coconut. mix well.
- Spoon the batter into cupcake or muffin cases in a muffin pan. I haven't been able to find a round muffin pan, so I use silicon muffin cases and place them on the halogen baking sheets that come with the accessory packs. You can comfortably fit 10 on the sheet.
- Place on the low rack and bake for 15–18 minutes. The cupcakes should be firm and spring back when touched. Place on a cooling rack to cool.
- Prepare the icing. Beat the butter and cream cheese together until soft. Gradually add the confectioners sugar and vanilla extract and beat until you reach the desired consistency—it should be glossy, thick, and lump-free. The best way of knowing whether you've added enough confectioners sugar is to taste the icing. It should taste sweet and creamy but not too buttery.

- If using silicon muffin cases, wait until the cupcakes are cool, then carefully pull away the sides of each case. Once the case is clear all the way around, turn it upside down and the cupcake should pop out.
- Put the icing into a icing bag. Start in the center of each cupcake and spiral outwards, covering the whole of the top, gently overlapping to avoid gaps.

SUITABLE FOR VEGETARIANS

½ cup butter
⅔ cup brown sugar
2 eggs, beaten
1 cup self-rising flour
2 teaspoons cinnamon
1 teaspoon coriander
1 large carrot, grated
⅓ cup raisins
½ cup unsweetened
  coconut flakes
⅓ cup sunflower
  kernals or
  mixed seeds
  (pumpkin, flaxseed,
  poppy, etc)

Vanilla Butter Icing
2 tablespoons butter
½ cup cream cheese
1¾–2 cups
  confectioners sugar
1 teaspoon vanilla
  extract or paste

Breakfast Muffins

I put this recipe together one day to try to get my family away from their chocolate-muffin addiction. They're delicious— especially when served warm with a little plain yogurt for an alternative breakfast treat. I use a seed mix, which contains omega-rich flax, sunflower, poppy, and pumpkin seeds, but feel free to experiment with your own versions.

- Preheat the halogen oven using the preheat setting, or set the temperature to 400°F.
- Cream the butter and brown sugar together in a mixing bowl until pale and fluffy. Add the eggs a little at a time and continue to beat well. Sift the flour and fold into the mixture gently.
- When thoroughly mixed, add the cinnamon, coriander, carrot, raisins, coconut, and seeds and mix well.
- Spoon the mixture into cupcake or muffin cases in a muffin pan. I haven't been able to find a round muffin tray, so I use silicon muffin cases and place them on the halogen baking sheets that come with the accessory packs. You can comfortably fit 10 on the sheet.
- Place on the low rack and cook for 15–18 minutes. The cakes should be firm and spring back when touched. Place on a cooling rack to cool.

Meal Planners

Meal planners are designed to make your life easier—and save you money. Until you plan your meals, you won't appreciate how much money you can save on your weekly grocery bills. It's estimated that over a third of our grocery shopping is wasted every week. If you plan your meals, you tend to buy only what you need and therefore avoid waste and unnecessary purchases.

Here is a selection of meal plans for your main meals only, complete with shopping lists to help get you started. I've included four weeks for those who eat meat and fish, and two weeks for vegetarians. The recipes included in this book appear in the meal planners in italics.

- While the cakes are cooling, prepare the icing. Beat the butter and cream cheese together until soft. Gradually add the confectioners sugar and vanilla extract and beat until you reach the desired consistency—it should be glossy, thick, and lump-free. The best way of knowing whether you've added enough confectioners sugar is to taste the icing. It should taste sweet and creamy but not too buttery.
- If using silicon muffin cases, wait until the cupcakes are cool, then carefully pull away the sides of each case. Once the case is clear all the way around, turn it upside down and the cupcake should pop out.
- Place the icing into an icing bag. Start in the center of each cooled cake and spiral outwards covering the whole of the cake top, gently overlapping to avoid gaps.
- Finish with a sprinkle of cinnamon and you're ready to serve.

SUITABLE FOR VEGETARIANS

Meat and fish meal planners

WEEK 1

Shopping list

1 whole chicken
1 red or Spanish onion
1 lemon
6½–9 lb potatoes
Seasonal vegetables for 4 meals
Salad for 2 meals
3 white onions
1 package of celery
¼ lb button mushrooms
¼ lb ham
1 x 10.75 oz can condensed cream
   of chicken or mushroom soup
1 package of ready-to-use puff pastry
1 package of ready-to-use phyllo pastry

1 lb 2 oz fish fillets
½ lb salmon fillets
1 lb cod fillets
¼ lb shrimp
3 oz Cheddar cheese
¼ lb Gruyère
2 oz (½ cup) grated Parmesan cheese
1¾ lb ground beef
1 chili
5 eggs
¾ lb spaghetti
1 x 14.5 oz can tomatoes
1 garlic bulb
1 lb baby leaf spinach

Pantry essentials

Olive oil	Cumin	Basil
Tarragon	Chili powder	Nutmeg
Paprika	Worcestershire sauce	Sesame seeds
Milk	Parsley	Coriander
Butter	Bread crumbs	Tomato paste
Flour	Sugar	Rolled oats
Mustard	Salt and pepper	Instant gravy

Meals • WEEK 1

Sunday: *Roast Chicken*, roasted potatoes, two seasonal vegetables, and gravy
- Buy a chicken that is slightly bigger than your needs, but make sure it fits in your halogen oven! You will then be able to strip it of meat (thighs, legs, breast and even turn the bird over to pull off the meat). Put the leftover meat to one side, ready for baking a chicken pie for tomorrow's dinner—plus, if you have any extra, you can use it to make sandwiches.
- When cooking the chicken, make room in the halogen for your roasted potatoes.

Monday: *Leftover Chicken Pie*, two vegetables, and mashed potatoes
- Prepare double the mashed potatoes and keep them in the refrigerator for tomorrow's fish pie.

Tuesday: *Creamy Fish Pie* and vegetables
- You already have the mashed potatoes prepared from yesterday's meal, so now all you have to do is prepare the fish pie.

Wednesday: *Spicy Meatballs in Rich Tomato Sauce*
- This can be prepared in advance, or why not double the recipe and freeze the second portion for another meal?
- Serve with spaghetti.

Thursday: *Spinach and Feta Pie* served with new potatoes and salad or vegetables
- This is a really light pie, so serve it with salad or fresh vegetables.

Friday: *Beef Burgers, Potato Wedges,* and salad
- Remember: you can double this recipe and freeze until needed.
- Place the potato wedges in the oven and, when you are ready to cook the burgers, you can leave the wedges on the low rack and broil the burgers on the top rack.

Saturday: *Cod, Egg, and Gruyère Bake*
- Serve with green vegetables.

Meat and fish meal planners

WEEK 2

Shopping list

Beef roast

4½ lb potatoes

4½ lb new potatoes

Seasonal vegetables for 4 meals

Seasonal salad for 2 meals

4 fish fillets

1 large bulb of fennel

1 bulb of garlic

2 onions

4 lemons

6 oz mushrooms

10 oz button mushrooms

10 oz sour cream

10 oz spaghetti or tagliatelle

Fresh herbs (e.g. parsley and dill)

4 salmon fillets

½ cup grated Parmesan cheese

2 leeks

1 bunch of spring onions

10 oz chicken pieces

4 chicken breasts

1¼ cups chicken stock

6 slices prosciutto

¼ lb French beans

10 oz crème fraîche

50g watercress

6 oz shrimp

1 lb 2 oz salmon

2 oz(about 2 cups) baby leaf spinach

½ package of ready-to-use puff pastry

8 oz cream cheese

1 large tomato

Pantry essentials

Dark brown sugar

Maple or light corn syrup

Horseradish

Butter

Olive oil

Tarragon

Dried onion

Dried chives

Red wine

White wine

Cornstarch

Paprika

Milk

Mustard

Sesame seeds

Cayenne pepper

Tabasco sauce

Salt and pepper

Mixed herbs

Meals • WEEK 2

Sunday: *Roast Beef and Horseradish,* roasted potatoes and two vegetables
- Buy a beef joint that is slightly bigger than your needs but make sure it fits in your halogen oven! Put the leftover meat to one side ready for Tuesday's stroganoff—plus, if you have any extra, you can use it to make sandwiches.
- When cooking the beef, make room in the halogen for your roasted potatoes.

Monday: *One Pot-roasted Fish, Fennel, and Red Onion*
- You could serve this with additional vegetables or potatoes if you wish.

Tuesday: *Beef Stroganoff*
- Serve with tagliatelle or spaghetti.

Wednesday: *Salmon and Herb Butter Parcels*
- Serve with new potatoes or *Cheese Crunch New Potatoes* and green vegetables.

Thursday: *Chicken and Mushroom Casserole*
- You could serve this with *Baked New Potatoes.*

Friday: *Salmon and Shrimp Puff Pie*
- Serve with salad or green vegetables.

Saturday: *Hot Stuffed Chicken with Prosciutto*
- Serve with *Fan Potatoes* and two vegetables.

Meat and fish meal planners

WEEK 3

Shopping list

1 leg of lamb
9 lb potatoes
2 sweet potatoes
Seasonal vegetables for 3 meals
Seasonal salad ingredients for 3 meals
1 garlic bulb
2 chilies
5 eggs
1 bunch of scallions (spring onions)
2 red bell peppers
6 strips of pancetta (or bacon)
1 jar of sun-dried tomatoes in oil
5 oz Parmesan cheese
3 red onions
1 onion
2 lb cod fillets
1 lemon
5 oz crème fraîche or sour cream
1 lb 2 oz bread flour

1 package active dried yeast
Chosen pizza toppings
4 carrots
1 lb ground lamb
¼ lb mushrooms
6 oz grated mature Cheddar
1 piece fresh root ginger
1 lime
4 lime leaves
2 sticks of lemongrass
1 x jar Thai curry paste
1 x 14 oz can of coconut milk
6 oz Greek yogurt
4 fish fillets
1 lb Thai Lime Rice
6 oz macaroni
8 strips of bacon
3 leeks

Pantry essentials

Rosemary (dried
  and fresh)
Fresh basil, oregano
  or thyme
Fresh coriander
Mixed dried herbs
Parsley

Butter
Milk
Brown sugar
Olive oil
Paprika
Red wine
Gravy
Worcestershire sauce

Farina
Cornstarch
Mustard
Bread crumbs
Rolled oats
Salt and pepper

Meals • WEEK 3

Sunday: *Roast Leg of Lamb with Roasted Vegetables*
- When cooking the lamb, make room in the halogen for your roasted vegetables.

Monday: *Mediterranean-style Tortilla*
- Serve with a green salad.

Tuesday: *Creamy Baked Cod*
- Serve with *Fan Potatoes* and vegetables.

Wednesday: *Homemade Pizza*
- Double the dough recipe and put the pizza bases in the freezer until needed.
- Choose your own toppings.
- Serve with *Potato Wedges* and salad.

Thursday: Shepherd's Pie
- A one-pot family favorite—serve it with vegetables and homemade gravy (or choose *Eco-warrior Pie* on page 134 for a vegetarian version, but you'll need to alter your shopping list).
- Double the recipe and freeze one pie for another meal.

Friday: *Thai Fish Bakes*
- Serve with steamed new potatoes or on a bed of rice and with your choice of vegetables.

Saturday: *Bacon, Leek, and Macaroni Cheese Bake*
- A filling and satisfying one-pot meal.

Meat and fish meal planners

WEEK 4

Shopping list

1 whole chicken
6½ lb potatoes
2 lemons
Seasonal vegetables for 3 meals
Seasonal salad for 3 meals
2 eggplants
5 red or Spanish onions
1 garlic bulb
4 peppers
1 lb lean ground beef
¼ lb mushrooms
¾ lb button mushrooms
4 tomatoes
2 oz grated mature Cheddar
4 mackerels
14 oz crème fraîche or sour cream
3 oz Gruyère cheese
4 boneless chicken breasts

1 package of pancetta (or bacon)
2 x 14.5 oz cans chopped tomatoes
2¼ lb new potatoes
14 oz canned tuna
½ lb corn (canned or frozen)
1 bunch of spring onions
Lasagne sheets
16 oz tomato purée
2 oz grated Parmesan
8 lean sausages
6 strips of bacon
1 sweet potato
12–14 cherry tomatoes
1 ball of mozzarella
   (or ¼ lb goat cheese)
1 lb 2 oz bread flour
1 package of active dry yeast

Pantry essentials

Paprika
Olive oil
Butter
Red wine
Tarragon

Mixed herbs
Milk
Nutmeg
Sun-dried tomato paste
Stock

Fresh basil
Fresh parsley
Salt and pepper
Sugar
Balsamic vinegar

Meals • WEEK 4

Sunday: *Roast Chicken,* roasted potatoes, and two veg
- Buy a chicken slightly bigger than your needs. If you have some left over, you can use it to make sandwiches.
- When cooking the chicken, make room for your roasted potatoes.

Monday: *Stuffed Eggplant*
- Double the tomato sauce recipe so that you have it ready for spaghett, lasagne, chili con carne, or as a topping for baked potatoes.

Tuesday: *Simple Mackerel Parcels*
- Serve with *Cheesy Dauphine Potatoes* and vegetables.

Wednesday: *Chicken Italiano*
- Serve with *Baked New Potatoes* and fresh seasonal vegetables.

Thursday: Tuna and Corn Lasagne
- Double the recipe and freeze one lasagne for another meal. Remember to label and date any frozen meals.
- Serve with *Potato Wedges* and salad.

Friday: *Sausage Casserole*
- Serve with mashed potato.

Saturday: *Upside-down Pizza Bake*
- Serve with a selection of salads.

Vegetarian meal planners

WEEK 1

Shopping list

1–2 butternut squash	4 eggplants
¼ lb mushrooms	3 red bell peppers
3 oz cashews	1 zucchini
¾ lb goat cheese	2–3 carrots
6½ lb potatoes	1 package of celery
5 red or Spanish onions	8 ripe tomatoes
1 garlic bulb	1 x 14.5 oz can chopped tomatoes
Seasonal vegetables for 3 meals	2 oz grated Parmesan
Seasonal salad for 3 meals	6 oz grated mature Cheddar
1 package ready-to-use phyllo pastry	5 eggs
14 oz feta cheese	1 bunch of scallions (spring onions)
1 lb baby leaf spinach	1 jar sun-dried tomatoes in oil
4½ lb new potatoes	1 x 14.5 oz can of tomatoes
1 lb 2 oz bread flour	2¼ lb sweet potatoes
1 package active dry yeast	1 lb vegetarian "ground beef"
Chosen pizza toppings	1¼ cups crème fraîche or sour cream

Pantry essentials

Butter	Fresh thyme	Rolled oats
Olive oil	Fresh bay leaves	Dried mint
Paprika	Mixed fresh herbs	Ground cinnamon
Salt and pepper	Sugar	Vegetable stock
Mixed herbs	Balsamic vinegar	Tomato paste
Nutmeg	Red wine	All-purpose flour
Sesame seeds	Bread crumbs	

Meals • WEEK 1

Sunday: *Butternut Squash Stuffed with Mushroom, Cashews, and Goat Cheese*
- Serve with *Fan Potatoes* and seasonal vegetables.

Monday: *Spinach and Feta Pie*
- Serve with new potatoes and green vegetables.

Tuesday: *Homemade Pizza*
- Serve with *Potato Wedges* and salad.

Wednesday: *Ratatouille and Feta Gratin*
- Serve with crusty bread and salad.

Thursday: *Sun-dried Tomato and Goat Cheese Frittata*
- Serve with a variety of salads.

Friday: *Vegetable Crumble*
- Serve with sweet potato mash and seasonal vegetables.

Saturday: *Vegetarian Moussaka*
- Double the sauce mixture because it can be frozen and used for spaghetti , lasagne, or even as a topping for baked potatoes.

Vegetarian meal planners

WEEK 2

Shopping list

4½ lb potatoes	1 cauliflower
4½ lb sweet potatoes	3 oz cashew nuts
4½ lbnew potatoes	4 oz natural yogurt
8 carrots	6 oz Parmesan cheese
4 leeks	Lasagne sheets
2 heads of broccoli	¼ lb mushrooms
1 lb 5 oz baby leaf spinach	1 tub of ricotta
16 tomatoes	5 red peppers
¾ lb mature Cheddar	12–15 cherry tomatoes
Seasonal veg for 4 meals	1 x 14.5 oz chopped tomatoes
1 x 15.5 oz can garbanzo beans	1 jar pasta sauce
1 package of tofu	1 small pumpkin or squash
5 onions	1 lemon
1 chili	1 piece fresh root ginger
1 package of celery	Crusty bread
6–8 wholewheat buns	Hummus
Salad for 3 meals	

Pantry essentials

Butter	Tomato paste	Balsamic vinegar
All-purpose flour	Garam masala	Sugar
Milk	Soy sauce	Vegetable stock
Mustard (including dry)	Bread crumbs	Mixed fresh herbs
Nutmeg	Rolled oats	Coriander
Sesame seeds	Self-rising flour	Salt and pepper
Olive oil	Fresh thyme	

Meals • WEEK 2

Sunday: *Eco-Warrior Pie*
- This can be a one-pot meal, or you can add some extra vegetables to accompany it.

Monday: *Tofu and Garbanzo Burgers*
- Serve with *Potato Wedges* or fries and salad.
- You can double this recipe and freeze the extra burgers, ready for another meal.

Tuesday: *Vegetable Cheesy Cobbler*
- This can be a one-pot meal—just add some extra seasonal vegetables or a green salad to accompany it.

Wednesday: *Spinach and Ricotta Lasagne*
- Serve with a selection of salads.

Thursday: *Roasted Tomato and Garlic Peppers*
- Serve with *Cheese Crunch New Potatoes.*

Friday: *Vegetable Crumble*
- Double the recipe and make one for the freezer, ready for another meal.

Saturday: *Roasted Pumpkin Soup*
- Double the recipe and store the extra soup in the refrigerator or freezer, ready for a snack or another meal.
- Serve with crusty bread and homemade hummus.

Index

68922915R00143